THE
BELGIANS AT

(With Translations of the Reports of the
Dutch and Belgian Commanders)

by

DEMETRIUS C. BOULGER

FOUR PLANS AND ILLUSTRATIONS

The Naval & Military Press Ltd

published in association with

FIREPOWER
The Royal Artillery Museum
Woolwich

Published by
The Naval & Military Press Ltd
Unit 10 Ridgewood Industrial Park,
Uckfield, East Sussex,
TN22 5QE England
Tel: +44 (0) 1825 749494
Fax: +44 (0) 1825 765701
www.naval-military-press.com

in association with

FIREPOWER
The Royal Artillery Museum, Woolwich
www.firepower.org.uk

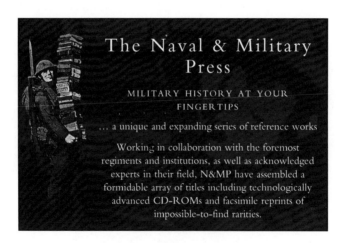

In reprinting in facsimile from the original, any imperfections are inevitably reproduced and the quality may fall short of modern type and cartographic standards.

Printed and bound by Antony Rowe Ltd, Eastbourne

COLONEL COENEGRACHT MORTALLY WOUNDED AT WATERLOO.

PREFACE

I AM indebted to the proprietors of the *Contemporary Review* for permission to republish my article on the Belgians at Waterloo which appeared in the number for May, 1900. I have made a few additions from the notes which I took during my researches in Brussels, and I have also interpolated some remarks on two articles on the same subject that appeared subsequently to mine in the *Nineteenth Century*.

I am under great obligations to Colonel F. de Bas, of the Dutch army, Director of the Archives of the War Department at the Hague, author of 'The Campaign of Prince Frederick of the Netherlands,' and himself one of the greatest living authorities on Waterloo, for the kindness with which he placed the manuscript treasures of his department at my disposal during a recent visit to the Hague. I am indebted to him for certified copies of all the reports which exist in the original among the records of the Dutch Government. These, with the exception of the report of the Prince of Orange, have never been printed in any language. The copying of these voluminous reports, which I give as *pièces justificatives*, entailed on his staff much labour. In my humble opinion their contents ought to silence the detractors of the Dutch-Belgians at Waterloo. The final proof in their favour remains, however, to be still discovered in the Duke of Wellington's own report, as Field-Marshal of the Netherlands army, and as Generalissimo of the Allied armies, to King William of June 21, 1815, which has never been discovered. I give Colonel de Bas this clue as an expression of my gratitude to him, and I hope he will follow it to a successful find.

Lastly, I must thank my friend Monsieur Albert de Bassompierre for the trouble he took in procuring from the Musée de Peinture, and the Musée des Estampes at Brussels, the copies of the contemporary pictures, prints and engravings which serve as illustrations to this volume.

DEMETRIUS C. BOULGER.

THE BELGIANS AT WATERLOO

'THE Belgic and Dutch troops behaved admirably,' said the first notice of the Battle of Waterloo which appeared in the *Times*. A letter in the London *Star* of June 23, 1815, affirmed that 'the Pays Bas regiments fought admirably.' In the *Times* leader of June 21, 1815, it was stated that at Quatre Bras 'the brave soldiers of the Low Countries were not slow to prove otherwise than by words that they were resolved to conquer or to die for their country and their Sovereign.' Lord Castlereagh, in the House of Lords in July, 1815, paid a tribute to 'the valour of the Belgians.' The Duke of Wellington, in his Order of December 9, 1815, at Paris, praised 'the conduct of the troops of the Netherlands throughout the campaign.' The Prussian General Pirch II., in a proclamation dated Namur, June 24, 1815, asserted that the Belgians had sustained their old brilliant reputation for courage, 'especially at the Battle of La Belle Alliance, where they fought with such intrepidity that they astonished the Allied armies.'

These extracts from contemporary testimony paint one side of the shield in a manner creditable to the conduct of the Belgians and to the candour of British and other chroniclers. They have, however, been thrust on one side and almost obliterated by the great number of English writers on the campaign of 1815 who, with one or two exceptions—prominent among them being the late Colonel Chesney—have spared no effort in convicting the Netherlands troops, and especially the Belgians, of cowardice and misconduct at both Quatre Bras and Waterloo. Siborne, Maclachlan and Alison are the three principal military authorities who accuse the Belgians of having acted as poltroons, and even as traitors, in those battles, and from them the smaller fry of writers who contribute to Books of Reference and Baedeker Guides have borrowed, and in borrowing have exaggerated, the worst charges of the works from which they derived all the knowledge they had of the subject, until at last the statement that 'the Belgians ran away at Waterloo' passes almost without challenge among Englishmen. Others great in politics or in romance formed their prejudices at the same source. Lord Derby, the Rupert of Debate, speaking in 1854 on the Foreign Enlistment Bill during the Crimean War, scornfully expressed the hope that at least 'the Belgians who ran away at Waterloo would not be enlisted.' Thackeray, in his great novel of 'Vanity Fair,' has personified the Belgian soldier of Quatre Bras in his Regulus Van Cutsum, and thinking that he was teaching history, when he was really confining himself more closely to the sphere of romance, allowed his pen to write the libel that 'when Ney dashed upon the advance of the allied troops, carrying one position after the other, . . . the squadrons among which Regulus rode showed the greatest activity in retreating before the French. Their movements were only checked by the advance of the British in their rear. Thus forced to halt, the enemy's cavalry had at length an opportunity of coming to close quarters with the "brave" Belgians before them, who preferred to encounter the British rather than the French, and at once turning tail, rode through the English regiments that were behind them and scattered in all directions. The regiment, in fact, did not exist any more.'

That is the other side of the shield, discreditable to the Belgians if true, but if untrue then to these English writers, and reflecting with tenfold force on Thackeray,* who has misled a thousand readers where the whole collective body of military historians have not deceived a hundred.

I do not propose to add to the controversial matter already existing on this subject. The Belgian Generals Renard and Eenens have in works of merit taken up the cudgels on behalf of their slandered countrymen. General Brialmont, in a weighty passage of his 'Life of Wellington,' has corrected some of the errors of Siborne and Alison. The Dutch military writers,

* One almost wonders if Thackeray had heard of the incident described by Count de St. Germain in his account of events at Brussels during the brief campaign. While waiting on the Place de la Monnaie and listening to the cannon at Quatre Bras, a wounded Brunswick officer in a black uniform rode across the Place and suddenly shot himself. His soldier-servant riding behind immediately followed his master's example.

Van Löben Sels, Knoop and De Bas, have contributed descriptions of the battle which are among the most valuable in any language, at the same time that their chief object has been to remove the reflection cast on the Netherlands troops by English writers. But I will endeavour to place before the reader in the form of a brief narrative, giving facts based on contemporary evidence that cannot be refuted and much of which will be new, an exact account of the part taken by the Belgians in the whole of the campaign. My object is to tear out of the picture of those memorable Hundred Days, and still more particularly of the campaign of Four Days from June 15 to 18, all the important details in which the Belgians played the chief or the sole part, and then to leave the reader to form his or her own opinion and conclusions from that record. I entertain no doubt, however, that it will refute the charges of cowardice brought against the Belgians, and establish the fact that they are entitled to claim a modest share and an honourable part in the glorious victory of Waterloo.

I

BEFORE THE CAMPAIGN

The subject naturally resolves itself into four divisions, and it is essential for the correct appreciation of the part taken by the Belgians in the campaign that certain historical facts bearing on their political existence and military organization at the moment it began should be first made clear.

Belgium, by the victory of Fleurus in 1794, became French, and in 1795 the Convention formally declared it part of the Republic. From that year until the beginning of 1814 the country enjoyed internal peace and external security under the protection of France. But it is a mistake to represent, as is generally done, the French rule as altogether popular among the Belgians. The great Flemish section of the nation, to whose enterprise and sterling qualities so much of the present prosperity and recent progress of the State is due, was then silent and passive, but in the opinion of even the French-speaking part of the Belgian community the security provided by the Republican, and after it by the Imperial, Government was bought at an excessive price by the heaviness of taxation, and by the constant levies for military service, while the closing of the Continent against British trade injured the commercial classes, and the arbitrary practice of sending the sons under compulsion to the military schools of France offended the aristocratic. Those few persons who were able to form part of Paris society under the Empire, or to attend the receptions at Laeken, may have worked up a factitious enthusiasm for the French connection, but the real sentiment of the Belgians was one of latent hostility and discontent under the rule of France.

In November, 1813, immediately after the Battle of Leipsic, Holland rose, under the patriotic Hogendorp, to recover its independence. The French garrisons were expelled, the Prince of Orange was summoned from England, and on December 1 he was proclaimed by the title of Prince Sovereign of the Netherlands. This event caused some excitement in Belgium, but there was no corresponding rising in that country, because there was no popular leader like Hogendorp, no national ruling family such as that of Orange, and, above all, because a considerable French army, under Marshal Macdonald and Generals Maison and Molitor, held the fortified towns. Moreover, the Dutch army, numbering 25,000 men, did not advance to support the general rising which its presence might have produced. The expulsion of the French from Holland was effected by a national rising. In Belgium it was brought about by the advance of the Prusso-Russian armies. On February 1, 1814, the Prussian advance-guard entered Brussels, and the citizens hailed the downfall of French authority with delirious joy, burning the French eagles on the Grand Place, and illuminating the city with the motto *Belgicæ felicitatis aurora*. Before the end of the month the French had lost the whole of the country with the exception of five fortified towns, which surrendered in the following April and May. In June, 1814, Belgium was united with Holland, and in February, 1815, the Vienna Congress sanctioned the creation of the Kingdom of the Netherlands. Napoleon landed from Elba on March 1, 1815, entering Paris on the 20th of the same month. The Prince of Orange, in consequence of Napoleon's reappearance, caused himself to be proclaimed King simultaneously at Amsterdam and Brussels on March 17, without waiting for the final mandate of the Powers.

Immediately after the expulsion of the French in the spring of 1814, steps were taken to raise a Belgian army. The Count de Murray and Baron Vincent, Austrian officers, were permitted to summon a levy of troops and to issue commissions. It was then thought that the former connection with Austria might be restored, and a very considerable section of the old nobility was in favour of this arrangement. A considerable number of Belgians who had served both as officers and men in the Walloon regiments of Austria joined the new army of their native country, while a still larger contingent was provided by Belgians who had served, and served well, too, under the eagles of Napoleon. There was thus provided a small nucleus of trained men and experienced officers. When the interregnum closed after three or four months with the extinguishing of Austrian hopes, another military element was imported into the organization of the national forces. The Prince of Orange, naturally enough, entrusted the higher posts and commands to Dutch officers who had served their military apprenticeship in the French army under their King Louis Napoleon and the Emperor. His Minister of War, for instance, was Marshal Janssens, who was notorious for the surrender of both the Cape and Java to the British; his Inspector-General of Infantry was Baron de Tindal, the creator of the Young Guard; and the ablest of his active commanders was Baron de Chassé, who in the Peninsula had gained against English troops the sobriquet of General Baïonnette. Events showed that these men were animated by a patriotic devotion to their newly-restored country and by loyalty to their King.

The troops raised in 1814, first by Austrian and then by Dutch officers, formed the Belgian regulars who took part in the Waterloo campaign. At first the infantry uniform was white, but on January 1, 1815, it was changed to blue, which was effected by the easy process of turning the coat inside out. The officers wore orange sashes, and the headgear was the English shako, with the initial W. in front. The Belgian regulars figured, of course, among the regiments of the Netherlands army, but while over 20,000 Dutch troops were raised, the total of the Belgians did not exceed 9,000 men at the beginning of the campaign. Between January and March 1, 1815—that is, before Napoleon's flight from Elba, and while the opinion was prevalent that peace would not be disturbed—several reviews of the new army were held, and the cavalry regiments, known as the Carabiniers, the 7th battalion recruited at Ghent, and the Croy —or 8th—Hussars under Prince Ferdinand de Croy, were always singled out for praise. This was not surprising, as the majority of the officers in those regiments had seen a good deal of active service. Some idea of their sentiments may be formed from the following speech of Colonel Knyff of the Carabiniers, when he, his officers, and the troopers took the oath to Prince William on January 6, 1815:

'MONSEIGNEUR,—The spokesman of the officers, sub-officers, and Carabiniers that I have the honour to command, I place at the feet of your Royal Highness the assurance of our boundless devotion. We have just sworn to live obedient and faithful; this oath was already engraved on our hearts. Your Highness can count on his regiment of Carabiniers; it will on all occasions give proof of fidelity and attachment to its Sovereign and its country. If the brave men who compose it knew under foreign flags how to merit the rewards due to their valour, what should not be expected of them when they are fighting for their own country and for a Prince who regards them with affection, and who is dear to them?'

The arrival of Napoleon in France altered the whole position, and among other consequences subjected the newly improvised and semi-organized army of the Netherlands to the severest tests of active warfare. It was also quickly realized that the forces raised were inadequate in numbers, and on April 1, 1815, the King issued a Proclamation stating that 'circumstances necessitating increase of forces to assure the independence of the country and its security against invasion,' a national militia of 25,000 men was to be formed. It is a little curious that a few days later Napoleon issued an invitation calling upon all Belgians who had served under him in the past to return to their old regiments. He remarked characteristically enough to one of his Marshals: 'In this way I shall get eight or ten thousand soldiers,' and it is very probable that this anecdote forms the basis of the legend of Belgian sympathy for France in 1815. The reply in the Brussels papers to the notice in the Paris *Moniteur* may serve to remove the impression. They said: 'When the sword is drawn, and if the Orange flag leads us in the field, they shall see on whose side there will be defection.' The French people, as well as their leader, were fully persuaded that the Belgians would at once rally to their side, but the former had nothing on which to base this expectation except their hopes. The London *Morning Chronicle* declared that the statement of Napoleon's landing having excited joy in Belgium, was 'an abominable calumny on a loyal and faithful people.' Even until the campaign began in earnest, Napoleon clung to the belief that the Belgian army would join him *en masse*. It was only after Quatre Bras that he gave up this belief, and in his rage incited his army to fresh efforts, with the promise of the pillage of Brussels.

Wellington was at Vienna when Napoleon landed from Elba, and he proceeded to the Low Countries to take over the command of the Allied army, reaching Brussels on the night of April 4-5. In May he was nominated Field-Marshal in the Netherlands army, and about the same date the King founded the military order of William as an incentive to his soldiers. From April until June Wellington was engaged in inspecting the Dutch and Belgian troops, while the British regiments were arriving from England. On several occasions Prince Blucher came to Brussels, and mention is made in the Brussels journals of a cavalry review held at Grammont on May 29. The British regiments on the ground were described as 'magnificent,' and two Belgian horse regiments were considered 'exceptionally good.' The arrangement for the campaign was that England was to provide 50,000 troops, but by June 18 only 33,000 had crossed the Channel, and of that number nearly 7,000 had not reached the front when the battle was fought. The total Netherlands army, Dutch and Belgian, ready for the campaign was officially given at 31,499 men, 7,450 horses, and 80 guns (48 6-pounders, 12 12-pounders, and 20 howitzers), but the effective strength did not exceed 28,000 men. The Netherlands troops were pushed forward gradually, from the beginning of the month of April, to the frontier, where they were to act as a screen. For two months and a half not a shot was fired between them and the French troops on the other side of the frontier, because the latter had been given strict injunctions not to molest the 'friendly' Belgians.

Although there was no fighting, several incidents occurred which will give the reader a correct idea of the temper of the Belgian people at the time. The Royal Family of France fled from Paris on Napoleon's approach, and Louis XVIII. established his Court at Ghent. His son, the Duc de Berri, when escaping, drove into Belgium in the neighbourhood of Ypres, and was closely pursued by a squadron of French cavalry, when a small detachment of the 7th Belgian Regiment, under Lieutenant Carondal, threw itself in their path and threatened to fire on the French troops. The commander of the latter attempted to effect his object by promising Carondal the Legion of Honour and a Captain's commission in the French army if he would surrender the Duc de Berri, but the offer was rejected, and the

French cavalry retired discomfited. Carondal received the Legion of Honour from Louis XVIII., but was killed at Waterloo. Another incident happened about the same time that is worth recalling. A Customs officer, named Picton, or more probably Piton, discovering that a French soldier with a very small force was removing twenty pieces of cannon from Dunkirk to Lille, collected a few men of his service and the Marechaussée, intercepted the guns and carried them off into Belgium. The third incident the memory of which I would revive occurred on June 15, after the first shot had been fired on the frontier. The younger Cambacérès and another French officer fell into the hands of the Belgians on that day, and were sent in a carriage under the guard of one trooper of the Marechaussée to Ghent. On the road Cambacérès offered the man a purse full of gold to permit him to escape. He received the reply : ' I am a Belgian soldier, not a traitor.'

II

Quatre Bras

Van Löben Sels, whose figures approach as nearly as possible to accuracy, gives the total of the Dutch-Belgian army at 23,440 infantry, 3,405 cavalry, 2,720 artillery, and 9 batteries of 8 guns each. Some of the Dutch regiments had had eighteen months' training, and some of the Belgian regiments had been under arms for twelve months, and in both, as explained, there was a large number of old soldiers and trained officers. Half the force, however, consisted of militia regiments, the bulk of which had only had a few months' training. Another military writer divides the Netherlands army as follows, which will give the reader some idea of the proportion of regular and militia regiments : Line infantry 8,684, Nassau Rifles 3,560, infantry militia 9,928, cavalry 2,466, artillery (regular) 2,000, artillery (militia) 1,534. This army early in April was formed in three divisions south of Brussels, with the idea of covering both the Mons and the Charleroi roads, while the Prussians under Blucher, who had his headquarters at Namur, were to watch the valley of the Meuse. At first the second division, under the command of General Baron de Perponcher, had its headquarters at Charleroi ; the first, under Prince Frederick of Orange, at Nivelles ; and the third, under Lieutenant-General Baron de

H.R.H. the Prince of Orange (afterwards King William II. of the Netherlands).

Chassé, at Braine le Comte. The Prince of Orange, who took the title on the assumption by his father of the style of King of the Netherlands, was in supreme command of the whole of the Dutch-Belgian force, and the chief of his staff was Baron de Constant de Rebecque. At Waterloo* the Prince, however, was entrusted by Wellington with the command of the centre of the Allied armies, and, to use the Duke's own words, ' so well directed the movements throughout all the day that from the commencement to the end I had not any need to send him a single order.' The troops were scattered over a very extensive stretch of country, and the two cavalry regiments—5th Light Horse and 6th Hussars—that fought at Quatre Bras were nearly 40 miles distant south of Mons and watching Maubeuge, when ordered the same morning to move with all speed to Nivelles.

The strategy and extraordinary celerity of Napoleon's movements need no further praise. On June 11 the Emperor left Paris, on the 14th he slept at Beaumont, and at three in the morning of the 15th, General Pajol surprised the Prussian cavalry at Ham-sur-Heure. At eight o'clock Charleroi was in the hands of the French, and about the same time there was a second cavalry fight at Courcelles. The advance of the French was so rapid and completely successful that it was not even believed. General Chassé received news from a vedette of the crossing of the Sambre by the French before mid-day, and at once sent off an express to Brussels, where the messenger arrived before three o'clock. I have since discovered that the first definite news of the French advance was obtained by General Van Merlen, who captured, late in the evening of June 14, a letter from a French officer, Baron Niel, giving details of the Emperor's advance, which Van Merlen sent to Chassé. The

* For clearness it may be well to repeat that the Belgian-Dutch Army consisted of three Infantry Divisions and one Cavalry Division. The First Infantry Division and the Indian Brigade, under the command of Prince Frederick, which guarded the Hal-Enghien position, took no part at Waterloo. The Second Division, commanded by Lieut.-General Baron de Perponcher, consisted of two brigades, the first commanded by Major-General Count de Bylandt, the second by Prince Bernard of Saxe-Weimar. The Third Division, under the orders of Lieut.-General Baron Chassé, also contained two brigades, the first commanded by Colonel Detmers, and the second by Major-General D'Aubremé. The Cavalry Division, under Lieut.-General Baron de Collaert, contained three brigades—one brigade of heavy cavalry, Carabiniers under the command of General Trip, and two brigades of light cavalry under Generals Ghigny and Van Merlen.

letter still exists at the Hague. The news was either not credited, or not acted upon until it could be discovered whether the French were advancing by Mons or by Charleroi, for Wellington persisted to the eleventh hour in believing from information he had received from Paris from ' a lady spy who had never misled him ' that the real French advance would be made by Mons. The Belgians were in no way involved in the cavalry skirmishing on the Sambre. Their part began on the 16th at Quatre Bras. It is not quite fair, however, to say this, because the fact of a stubborn resistance being even possible at Quatre Bras was entirely due, not to Wellington, but to the action in the evening of the 15th of certain Netherlands officers in high command. Gneisenau has made this quite clear, but the following evidence will support his conclusions.

One brigade of Perponcher's division, under Prince Bernard of Saxe-Weimar, was stationed between Genappe and Frasnes and about Quatre Bras, the cross-roads where the Nivelles-Namur route cuts the chaussée from Brussels to Charleroi. The brigade was composed of four battalions, with one battery and no cavalry. The bulk of the brigade was on the slopes below Quatre Bras, holding the wood of Boussu and the farm of Grand Pierrepont behind the stream of Germinecourt, which is nothing more than a ditch. One battalion of riflemen, with the battery, was placed in advance on the heights where is now the railway-station above the little village of Frasnes. The distance from Frasnes station to the cross-roads is as nearly as possible two miles. At 6.30 in the evening of June 15, the advanced battalion, with the guns in support, was attacked by the French cavalry. It slowly retired on Quatre Bras in perfect order and without suffering any material loss. At nine in the same evening, Prince Bernard wrote the following letter to his divisional commander, General de Perponcher, at Nivelles: 'I must confess to your Excellency that I am too weak to hold out here long. The two Orange-Nassau battalions have French guns, and each man has only ten cartridges. The Volunteer Chasseurs have carabines of four different calibres and only ten cartridges per carabine. I will defend as well and as long as possible the posts entrusted to me. I expect an attack by the enemy at daybreak. The troops are animated by the best spirit. The battery has no infantry cartridges.'

Those were the conditions under which the important position of Quatre Bras was to be held against the corps of Ney, who at daybreak on the 16th had 16 infantry battalions, 5 cavalry regiments, and 50 guns at his immediate disposal. Fortunately, he had no knowledge of the weakness of the force in front of him.

Orders had been given by the Prince of Orange, by command of the Duke of Wellington, to concentrate the division at Nivelles—that was to guard the Mons road and to leave the Charleroi road uncovered. Baron de Constant de Rebecque, chief of the Prince's staff, is entitled to the credit of altering the point of concentration from Nivelles to Quatre Bras, and General de Perponcher to that of ignoring the original order, and, in response to Prince Bernard's letter, of moving in person with his remaining brigade, that of De Bylandt, to Quatre Bras. At the same time, De Constant ordered the 1st Cavalry Brigade, under Ghigny, and the three regiments of Carabiniers, under Trip, to move nearer the scene of action, while Van Merlen's light cavalry brigade was ordered to march with all speed from near Maubeuge to Nivelles, and thence to Quatre Bras. In his letter to the Prince of Orange, at Brussels, dated ten o'clock in the evening of June 15, from Braine le Comte, De Constant thus explains and justifies what he had done:

'At this moment Captain Baron de Gagern has arrived from Nivelles, reporting that the enemy has shown himself at Quatre Bras. I have thought it my duty to take it on myself to instruct General de Perponcher to support his second brigade with the first, and to warn the third division and the cavalry in order to support them if necessary.'

At 11.30 the same night General de Chassé received the order to move with the third division from Fay to Nivelles, but as this corps took no part at Quatre Bras, its further movements need not be followed, especially as they are fully set forth in the Reports in the Appendix. Van Merlen received the summons soon after sunrise, on June 16, at St. Symphorien aux Bergen, and arrived at Quatre Bras with his two cavalry regiments—the 6th Hussars and the 5th Light Horse—a little before half-past three o'clock in the afternoon.

To return now to Prince Bernard. The French did not attack at daybreak, nor throughout the morning. At ten o'clock the greater part of Bylandt's brigade came up, but the 7th Belgian Regular Line Regiment, forming part of it, did not arrive on the scene until half-past three o'clock, when it was thrown into the wood of Boussu, part of which it held throughout the remainder of the afternoon. Up to three o'clock, then, the force holding Quatre Bras was exclusively Dutch and Belgian. It was composed only of infantry with two batteries, or 16 guns—one, Dutch, under the command of Van Byleweldt; and the other, Belgian, under Stievenaer. Of the eight battalions of infantry, three were militia. The Prince of Orange, it should be stated, arrived at Quatre Bras at seven in the morning of the 16th, and took command of the position.

Ney, having waited for Foy's division, did not begin the attack until about two o'clock, but a quarter of an hour later the action had become hot. One Dutch battalion was caught, after suffering a good deal from the French guns, by the enemy's cavalry, and only escaped destruction by rallying in the buildings of the farm of St. Pierre. Things looked so desperate at three o'clock that the Prince of Orange led a battalion to the charge, had his horse shot under him, and narrowly escaped being taken prisoner. It was immediately after this incident that the approach of the cavalry brigade under Van Merlen was signalled along the Nivelles road. At that moment the battle was practically lost. The English had not arrived, Ney was in the very act of being reinforced by Prince Jerome and his division, and nothing could gain the half-hour's respite still needed to save the position before the English troops could come up except some desperate measure. The arrival of the Dutch-Belgian cavalry brigade of Van Merlen gave the Prince of Orange the means of taking it, and he did not hesitate a moment in doing so. It was his last throw. Ten minutes later, and the Perponcher division would have been ousted from Quatre Bras.

The brigade of Van Merlen consisted of the 6th Hussars, a Dutch regiment, and the 5th Light Horse, or Dragoons, a Belgian corps. The total strength of the two regiments is given at 1,100, but it is not probable that more than a thousand men took part in the charge itself, and the official return gives the 5th Light Horse at only 400 sabres. It will be recollected that these troops had marched nearly forty miles, and the emergency was so great that not a moment could be spared to breathe their horses. The charge was necessarily not made in the most perfect order, and is described as a charge *en fourrageur*. The 6th Hussars happened to be leading. They were at once formed up and ordered to charge the enemy. They never seem to have had a chance, for as they charged down on the French infantry they were greeted with several withering volleys from

General Van Merlen.

the French guns, and were then taken in flank by the French 6th Hussars under Colonel de Faudoas. The Belgian regiment then charged in support of its brother corps. It is said that the French recognised them as Belgians, and called on them to ride through their ranks and join their old colours. The story is probably without any foundation—a mere assumption based on the fact that there were in the Belgian regiment officers and men who had served under Napoleon. However, the proposal, if made, was spurned, and a fierce mêlée ensued. The Belgian regiment gave a good account of itself, and retired on the main position. Unfortunately, the British infantry had just arrived, and mistaking the Belgian for French cavalry, through similarity of uniform, fired upon this regiment, inflicting some loss before the mistake was discovered.

That is an exact account of the Dutch-Belgian cavalry charge at Quatre Bras against a far superior French cavalry force, viz., two regiments, one from each of the brigades Wauthier and Hubert, of the Piré division, and of the conduct of those Hussars and Dragoons whom Thackeray maligned in the memorable passage in 'Vanity Fair.' The Van Merlen charge alone enabled the Prince of Orange to maintain his ground until Picton arrived at half-past three with his division. In that charge the 6th Hussars lost three officers killed (Heiders, Wynberger and Verhellow), 141 men killed, 64 men wounded, and six officers wounded (Jacobi, Paauw, Deebetz, Rendorp, Van Utenhove, and Wolfs), or 214 in all. The 5th Light Horse lost two officers wounded, 81 men killed, and 74 men wounded, or 157 in all. The wounded officers were Colonel De Merx, who received four wounds, and Captain Van Remortere, an ex-officer of the French army, who fought and wounded his former maréchal des logis. Curiously enough, the two met again a week later among the wounded in a hospital at Brussels. Among officers especially distinguished in this charge were Captains Brion and Crooy. Both were ex-officers of the Imperial army, and the latter killed a French officer at Quatre Bras with his own hand. To complete the evidence refuting the charge of cowardice and running away at Quatre Bras against these two regiments—the only Dutch and Belgian cavalry present—it may be added here that both were at Waterloo. They were stationed with the other Netherlands cavalry on Mont St. Jean. The Belgian regiment—the 5th Light Horse—made at least one charge there, and the gallant Major-General Van Merlen, who passed scatheless through Quatre Bras, was killed at its head, while the 6th Hussars, under Colonel Boreel, took part in the final charges of Vivian. The Belgian battery of Stievenaer also suffered heavily. The commanding officer was himself killed, two of the guns were lost, one gun was disabled, and all the horses of three others were killed, for which reason they were left on the battlefield. The two remaining guns were preserved by Lieutenant Winzinger, and took part in the Battle of Waterloo on the extreme left of the Allied position. The total loss of the Netherlands troops at Quatre Bras is given at 667 men of the infantry and artillery, and 371 of the cavalry, but the returns for this battle are admitted to be very defective, and the real loss was probably greater.

Wellington, in a letter to a friend, described Quatre Bras as 'a desperate battle, in which I was successful,' but the credit of holding the position against overwhelming odds and far superior troops up to half-past three belongs to the Netherlands division of De Perponcher, serving under the personal command of the Prince of Orange. The following is the official report of the Prince of Orange to his father, the King of the Netherlands:

'HEADQUARTERS AT NIVELLES,
'*June* 17, 1815, 2 *o'clock in the morning.*

'The Prussian Army was attacked on the 15th very early in the morning in its positions, which it abandoned, and retired from Charleroi by Gosselies to the neighbourhood of Fleurus. As soon as I had knowledge of that attack I gave the necessary orders to the army corps under my command. The result of what had happened to the Prussian Army was that the battalion of Orange-Nassau, which occupied the village of Fraisne (*sic*) with a battery of light artillery, was attacked on the 15th at five in the evening. The troops maintained themselves in the position on the heights of that village at a short distance from the road called Quatre Bras. Skirmishing ceased at this point at eight in the evening. As soon as I was informed of the attack I ordered the third division, as well as the cavalry and two English divisions, to advance to Nivelles, and the second division to support the position of Quatre Bras. Only a part of the second division could move at once, seeing that the brigade of Major-General de Bylandt could not leave Nivelles before the arrival of the other divisions there.

'The fire of the tirailleurs commenced yesterday morning at five o'clock at this point, and we carried it on on both sides till twelve o'clock without result. About two o'clock the attack became fierce, especially by the cavalry and artillery. The brigade of light cavalry under General Van Merlen could not arrive till nearly four o'clock; I had before this no cavalry to oppose to the enemy. Seeing how important it was to preserve the position on the heights of the road called Quatre Bras, I was fortunate enough to hold it against an enemy very superior in every respect. Having been attacked by the two

The Prince of Orange leading the Charge at Quatre Bras.

army corps of D'Erlon and Reille, and having succeeded in holding them in check, the Duke of Wellington had enough time to reunite sufficient forces to baffle the designs of the enemy. The result of this attack was that after an obstinate fight, which continued till nine in the evening, we not only stopped the enemy, but even drove him back.

'The Prussian Army, also attacked yesterday, maintained its principal posts, and it is beyond doubt the chief's determination with united forces to attack along the whole line. Our troops bivouacked on the field of battle, whither I am now going, seeing that it is highly probable that Napoleon will seek to-day to execute his project of yesterday. The Duke of Wellington has assembled there as many troops as he could.

'I experience a keen pleasure in being able to inform your Majesty that his troops, the infantry and artillery particularly, fought with much courage.

'Circumstances not allowing of my receiving the reports of the different corps concerning their losses, it is impossible for me to inform you of it, but I shall have the honour of doing so as soon as possible.

'WILLIAM PRINCE OF ORANGE.'

Carmichael Smith, an English officer present, as well as General Gneisenau, whose mistrust of Wellington must not blind us to his great authority, praised 'the steadiness of the Belgian-Netherlands troops,' and the account of Quatre Bras may be concluded with the following description from the London *Star* of June 21, 1815:

'The rebels (*i.e.*, the French) attacked with fury the Brunswickers and the Belgians, who, although very inferior in number, received them with the greatest intrepidity. An incident covered the Belgians with glory and their adversaries with shame. The rebels, hoping to find among the former a perfidy equal to their own, advanced towards them crying out to them to join their beloved Emperor, but this appeal was rejected with derision, and the brave soldiers of the Low Countries were not slow to prove otherwise than by words that they were resolved to conquer or to die for their country and their Sovereign.'

III

WATERLOO

The Netherlands troops had no part in the skirmishing of the 17th, General de Perponcher's division retiring with the British infantry on Mont St. Jean. At the same time the third division, under Baron de Chassé, which had advanced to Nivelles, received orders to march for the same point. The remaining or First Netherlands Division, under Prince Frederick of Orange, was stationed at Tubise—three and a half miles in front of Hal—with its left at Clabbeck and Braine le Chateau, only ten miles from the scene of the coming battle. Prince Frederick had under him as brigadiers Generals Stedman (Dutch) and Anthing, and the English officer General Sir C. Colville was also with this force, which numbered between 12,000 and 15,000 men. Van Löben Sels gives its strength at 12,700 men, 2,906 horses and 40 guns. It contained some of the best Dutch troops, including the Indian brigade specially raised for the reoccupation of Java; but as Wellington did not allow it to move from Hal, it took no part in the Battle of Waterloo, although it had a prominent share in the operations in the North of France subsequent to the battle.

The Netherlands forces that took part in the Battle of Waterloo were the Perponcher and Chassé infantry divisions, with four complete batteries of 32 guns, and the two guns saved as already described from Quatre Bras by Winzinger. To these last two guns was added a howitzer, and the three were placed in a position on the extreme left above Smohain and La Haye, supporting the brigade of Prince Bernard of Saxe-Weimar. There was also a cavalry division, under General Baron Collaert, composed of three brigades under Generals Ghigny, Trip and Van Merlen. The reduced strength of the Perponcher division was 7,500 men, with the battery of Van Byleweldt. It was placed in the left wing of the Allied army, and attached to the division under Sir Thomas Picton. One of the two Orange-Nassau rifle battalions was taken from the division and stationed in the wood of Hougoumont, so that the total strength on the left was about 6,700 men. The third division, under General Baron de Chassé—the General Baïonnette who had specially distinguished himself at Talavera and at the Col de Maja, where he had saved D'Erlon, and who fifteen years later became famous as the defender of Antwerp, which he held with 6,000 Dutch troops against 70,000 French—numbered 6,669 men, its brigades being commanded by Detmers and Aubremé. Attached to this division were two batteries or 16 guns, one (horse battery) of 6-pounders and one of 12-pounders. The position assigned to this division by Wellington was at Braine l'Alleud, in the rear of his extreme right. The Detmers brigade was first stationed at that village, while that under Aubremé was further west at the farm of Vieux Foriez, that is to say, at a greater distance from the field of battle. The total strength of the cavalry division under Collaert numbered 3,646, including the battery attached to it of horse artillery. The first brigade, under Baron Trip, was composed of the three Carabinier regiments—heavy cavalry—the 1st and 3rd being Dutch and the 2nd Belgian, mainly recruited in Brussels. The second brigade, under Baron Ghigny, contained two regiments, the 4th Dragoons (Dutch) and the 8th Croy Hussars (Belgian). The third brigade, under Van Merlen, consisted of the remains of the two regiments that fought at Quatre Bras, together equal to one regiment. Attached to the cavalry division was one battery of Netherlands horse artillery, under Captain Petter. The first position of the Netherlands cavalry was in front of the farm of Mont St. Jean, on the right of the chaussée and directly behind the English heavy cavalry. The exact position of the Netherlands troops may be thus summed up. The third division (Chassé) was in reserve behind the second line on the right, the cavalry was in the rear of the centre, and the Perponcher division was in the most exposed point on the left. Naturally the last experienced the first shock and test, and, dividing the narrative into the fortunes of the three separate bodies enumerated, priority in point of time belongs to that under Perponcher. It is also the more important, for the charge of absolute cowardice, so far as Waterloo is concerned, against the Belgians relates to this body alone.

The Bylandt brigade of this division was also the portion of this force more particularly involved, because that under Prince Bernard, whether from its losses at Quatre Bras, or from the inferiority of its weapons, as mentioned in that Brigadier's letter of June 15, was posted in a less exposed position further to the left, opposite Frichermont. But Bylandt's brigade was placed very much in the front on the ground south of the Wavre road —frequently called chaussée d'Ohain—while Picton's brigade was stationed north of the same road and somewhat protected by a hedge. At least, this is the generally accepted opinion, although it must now be modified, because the report of Van Zuylen van Nyevelt leaves not a shadow of doubt that Bylandt's troops were withdrawn behind the road into line with the English before the action commenced. There is no doubt, however, that the Belgian-Dutch were at first placed in the point of danger and honour at this part of Wellington's position on the height of Mont St. Jean. They were also the very Belgian-Dutch troops who had fought at Quatre Bras, and associated with them was Picton's own division, the very force which had reached Quatre Bras just in time to save the day. If they had behaved like cowards on the 16th, would they have been put there on the 18th? Yes, some may say, in order to prevent them running away again. But if they had run away on the 16th, or even on the 17th, would they not have run away to sufficient purpose to render it impossible for the British commander to station them where he did? Yet the returns are conclusive that Perponcher's division was in full strength on the ground, over 7,000 men out of an original 8,000 before Quatre Bras.

Count de Bylandt's brigade consisted of five battalions, two regulars and three militia. The regulars were the 7th of the Line and the 27th Chasseurs. The militia were the 5th, 7th and 8th, and of these the 5th had suffered so heavily at Quatre Bras that it was placed in reserve behind the other militia regiments. The four other battalions named stood in a line, the two regular regiments adjoining Kempt's brigade, while the militia regiments touched the Highlanders—the 92nd and 42nd—under Pack. They were young, inexperienced troops—more than half of them militia—and they were put in juxtaposition with the picked troops of Wellington's army. But of those five battalions, only one—the 7th—was Belgian, the others were Dutch. A good enough case can be made out for the vindication of Bylandt's brigade, but that for the only Belgian regiment attached to it is still stronger.

Several writers, and among them Hooper and Shaw Kennedy, have said that the exposure of Bylandt's brigade cannot be explained, but of course when Wellington put it south of the road it was not known that Napoleon would crown the opposite ridge with the 80 pieces of artillery that covered D'Erlon's attack on our left. That formidable collection of guns, half the total number that Napoleon employed against Wellington, directed its fire from a distance of 700 yards on Bylandt's force across the valley up which D'Erlon's column of 16,000 men moved to the attack. The decimation of the force was only averted by its timely withdrawal behind the road. If militia regiments were unsteady under those circumstances there would be no ground for surprise. It is on record that Picton's A.D.C. said to him at that moment that the Belgians would be sure to run before the crushing force bearing down on them, and Picton is affirmed to have replied: 'No, no! They will bite there a little in any case.' It is impossible to say exactly what took place, but as could scarcely have been different with the best troops under such circumstances, the Netherlands regiments seem to have been forced

The Prince of Orange leading the Charge at Waterloo.

back by the weight of the French column, but as they had been withdrawn from their most advanced position the distance of this retirement was not as great as is assumed by English writers. Captain Arthur Gore, a very careful authority, who translated Craan's detailed account of the forces and successive movements at the battle, and who made known his admirable plan of the battlefield, gave the following description a few days later. He wrote: 'The Belgian (correctly Netherlands and four-fifths Dutch) division gave way because they could not resist that formidable mass, and retired with great loss. They immediately re-formed behind the 5th Battalion and again advanced.' Bearing in mind the relative position of the four Netherlands battalions, it is sufficiently clear that the troops who re-formed behind the 5th Militia Battalion were themselves the Dutch militia, numbered 7th and 8th.

The German writer, Major Danmitz, says that 'the division was broken by the charge, but subsequently and soon rallied and continued to aid Picton's division.' The English writer, who is known as the historian of Picton's division, is very critical in his remarks on the conduct of Bylandt's brigade, but he goes on to 'exonerate a Belgian Colonel and his little body of troops, *who held firm under the heaviest fire throughout the day*.' There can be no question that the little body of troops was the 7th Regiment—the only Belgian corps at this point—and the Belgian Colonel was Van den Sanden. The following very modest account of what took place, written by the Adjutant of the 7th —afterwards Colonel—Scheltens, will carry the conviction that that regiment did not even give ground. I have left in his information as to the regiment's subsequent movements, and it will be noted from the reference to '*behind the road*' in the first line that General Renard's statement as to Bylandt's brigade having been drawn back from its most advanced position is confirmed. The Dutch official writers are borne out by Zuylen van Nyevelt's report—Appendix—in their assertion that Perponcher, on his own responsibility, sent an order *at mid-day* for the retirement behind the hollow road. This was before the French batteries began firing. It is therefore clear from the evidence that the Bylandt brigade was withdrawn from the ground which under a mistaken view of the facts it was denounced for having abandoned. Scheltens' statement reads as follows: 'The battalion remained lying down *behind the road* until the head of the French column was at the distance of a pistol-shot. The line then received the order to rise and commence firing. The French column, which was crossing the hollow road, committed the fault of halting in order to reply to our fire. We were firing at such close quarters that Captain L'Olivier received the wad with the ball of a rifle in his wound. The fire of the English very soon enveloped the column, which endeavoured to deploy instead of pushing on. The English cavalry arrived to take part in the fray. It passed like a whirlwind along the wings of our battalion, several of our men being knocked down by the horsemen. The battalion, which had to cease firing, for the cavalry were in front, immediately crossed the road and advanced. The enemy, taken in flank by Picton's regiments, and in reverse by the cavalry, was compelled to retreat, leaving behind a great many prisoners. The battalion then took up again its first position, where it remained to the end of the battle. There was no further serious attack on this side, only fighting between *tirailleurs*. In the evening we bivouacked on the very position we had held throughout the day. We were no more than 300 men all included; all the rest had been killed or wounded in this terrible affair—it was about half the effective. In a review held in the Bois de Boulogne by the Duke of Wellington, that General stopped before the battalion and complimented it on its fine conduct at Waterloo.'

I think that account, taken into consideration with the other evidence, will decide what the 7th regiment—the only Belgian corps in Bylandt's brigade—did at Waterloo. It did its duty. According to the official return the 7th captured two eagles and lost 236 killed and wounded out of 543, having previously lost at Quatre Bras 100 killed and as many more wounded. Two officers were killed at Waterloo, Lieutenant Carondal, the rescuer of the Duc de Berri, being one. Colonel Van den Sanden was wounded in several places, but he resumed his command a month later, on July 16, in France. The 7th Regiment naturally became the heroes of the Belgian populace, and the following incident is described on the authority of the *Times* of June 27, 1815. It is affirmed that during the battle the 7th rescued the Prince of Orange, who freely exposed his person, and that the Prince threw the star of the order he was wearing among them, exclaiming, 'My children, you have all of you deserved it!' The troops snatched it up and affixed it to their regimental flagstaff. Literally true or not, the great painter of the day, the Chevalier de Odevaere, made this incident the central point in his Waterloo picture.

ODEVAERE'S PICTURE OF WATERLOO.

I have finished with the 7th Belgian Regiment at Waterloo, but before passing on I have one word to say on behalf of Bylandt. The Perponcher division lost at Waterloo nearly 1,500 killed, missing, and wounded, in addition to the 667 men it lost at Quatre Bras. The full return for the two battles reads: 12 officers killed, 1,024 men killed and missing; 66 officers wounded, and 1,039 men wounded. That is a proportional loss of more than one man in four. To complete the story it only remains to add that General de Perponcher had three horses killed under him, and that General Bylandt was wounded. The Colonels of the three militia regiments were all wounded, and also Colonel Van den Sanden, of the 7th.

The next portion of the battle to be examined is that in which the Netherlands cavalry played a part. No serious reflections have been cast on this body of troops, and Wellington, in his admittedly bald and incomplete account of the battle, specifically mentions Trip, the Major-General in command of the Carabinier Brigade.

Sir Herbert Maxwell, in an article in the *Nineteenth Century* for September, 1900, corrected an error which I committed at this point in stating that the Duke of Wellington made no reference in his report to the immortal charge of the Union Brigade. I admit the error, and at the same time I may correct a mistake committed by Sir Herbert himself on the page of his own article containing the rectification mentioned. He calls the Cumberland Hussars 'Netherlander Volunteers.' They had nothing to do with the Netherlands. They were Germans, forming part of the Hanoverian army, and at least one of the officers, the Colonel in command, was an Englishman.

Sir Herbert Maxwell's article called forth a virulent protest from the pen of Mr. C. Oman, in the following *Nineteenth Century*, against the former's effort to do justice to our Allies at Waterloo. The virulence of this protest was worthy of Siborne himself, and of Siborne when he wrote his first edition, before he felt constrained to add the qualification about the conduct of Bylandt's brigade, which figures as a note on pages 396 and 397 of the later editions of his 'Waterloo Campaign.'

I only propose to give one illustration of the value of Mr. Oman's opinions. The chief point which this writer attempts to make in order to establish the cowardice of the Dutch-Belgians is that, in the lists of 'killed,' the 'missing' are included, and he does not hesitate to interpret 'missing' as 'absconded to the rear.' Let it be stated here, to remove all possibility of misunderstanding, that in the official returns of the losses of the Netherlands army distinction is carefully made between 'killed' and 'missing,' as well as between 'severely wounded' and 'slightly wounded.' It will be evident to the most ordinary intelligence that if the 'missing' in the Dutch-Belgian returns are to be treated as fugitives or absconders—in plainer words as cowards—the same interpretation must be applied to the 'missing' in the English and Prussian armies. Mr. Oman evidently forgot that there was a 'missing' column also in the returns of those two armies, whose courage has never been questioned, and that his argument might be turned with deadly effect against himself.

It is necessary, in the first place, to establish the meaning of the term 'missing.' In military language these are men who do not answer the roll-call at the end of the day, and whose fate it has not been possible to prove. There may be in the list of missing, killed and wounded left on the battlefield, as was the case at Quatre Bras, also, and more especially, prisoners and, finally, men who fled from their duty.

One of the English regiments that most distinguished itself at Waterloo—the 2nd Life Guards—had in the battle as many missing as killed and wounded put together (17 killed, 41 wounded, and 97 missing). Another regiment, the 1st or King's Dragoon Guards, had a great many more missing than killed, and nearly as many missing as killed and wounded together. The exact figures for this regiment were 43 killed, 104 wounded, and 128 missing.

How would Mr. Oman be able to reply if some foreign critic, imitating his bad example, were to asperse the missing of those gallant regiments and call them 'absconders'?

In the same way no one has ever thought of disputing the valour of the 1st Prussian Corps (Von Ziethen), and yet its losses from June 15 to July 3, 1815, were made up of 7,978 killed and wounded, and 6,422 missing ! (Consult Scheltema, 'Delaaste veldtocht von Napoleon-Bonaparte.')

If the enumeration is made from the official documents of the losses in killed and wounded alone, excluding the missing, of the Dutch-Belgians on June 18, the following result is arrived at :

The total effective Dutch-Belgian strength present in the battle of the 18th was 17,717 men. The loss of this force in killed and wounded alone was about 1,900 men, or approxi-

THE PRINCE OF ORANGE WOUNDED AT WATERLOO.

mately 11 per cent.; but it should not be lost sight of that one of the divisions—Chassé's—was only engaged towards the close of the day. The Perponcher division alone lost between 12 and 13 per cent. in killed and wounded, and the cavalry division 18 per cent.

As the reader can see, the percentage of losses suffered by the Dutch-Belgian contingent was high. An army cannot be accused of cowardice when its component parts suffered losses of 10, 12 and 18 per cent. from the enemy's fire, and when it bivouacked on the battlefield.

As to the 'missing' in the Dutch-Belgian army, the official reports show that the total returns of missing for each of the divisions are in every case appreciably less than the killed and wounded, and in no case did they exceed 7 per cent. of the effective. All the same, it must not be lost sight of that the army was one of very recent formation, not exceeding in any instance eighteen months, and in many cases the men had only had ten months' training. It may also be noted that the second and third divisions contained nine battalions of Dutch National Militia out of a total of twenty-two battalions.

Moreover, the two instances given with regard to the English and the Prussians prove that troops may behave valiantly and yet show a considerable number of 'missing.'

The second and third Netherlands divisions had a relatively high list of 'missing'; but it should be remembered that, so far as concerns the second division, it was engaged throughout the whole day, although it had already been very exposed and suffered much at Quatre Bras. Of the two brigades forming it, one, that of de Bylandt, had been particularly tried, and yet had to receive the rudest shock, while the other, that of Saxe-Weimar, fought over a wide extent of ground. The latter was placed on the extreme left, isolated, and scattered in outlying posts, and towards the end of the day it was also mixed up with the Prussian corps of Bulow; consequently some confusion was inevitable.

As to the Chassé division, it was also distributed along an extended front. It had also to manœuvre on the battlefield, and proceeded from the extreme right to the centre in order to take part in repulsing the attack of the French Guard. Under these conditions, it would inevitably have more 'missing' than troops massed at a fixed position who were not called upon to manœuvre.

Finally, the courage of any force should not be gauged by the number of 'missing' at the end of the day, for this number depends on the situation in which the force is found, whilst the losses suffered by the enemy's fire provide a sure basis for a just appreciation.

The case previously cited of the 2nd Life Guards, which had more missing than killed and wounded, and which beyond question distinguished itself in a pre-eminent degree, is really a perfectly natural phenomenon. The more troops are exposed, the more obstinate their action, the more 'missing' might then be expected amongst them. A force which acts weakly, and gives ground after a moderate effort, retires with almost all its men. But if the force is energetic as far as being a constituted body, then only can individual failings, the errors of direction committed by some parts of it which stray and only rejoin later on, through the confusion inseparable from an engagement pushed to the furthest point, be ascertained.

Mr. Oman is evidently possessed by the strange idea that, in order to establish the gallantry of the English army at Waterloo, it is necessary to show that the other troops under Wellington behaved like cowards. I am no asperser of my own kinsman Sir Colquhoun Grant, who had five horses killed under him in the battle, because I say that Van Merlen died a soldier's death, and that Chassé took a prominent part in deciding a critical phase of the battle.

The brunt of the cavalry fighting fell on the Carabiniers, of which the first and third regiments were Dutch, and the second regiment, under Colonel De Bruyn, Belgian. They took part in the successive charges of the Heavy British Brigade, with the exception perhaps of the first charge made in support of the Union Brigade, although the Dutch writers state positively that Trip supported Ponsonby. At that time they were placed in reserve behind our Household regiments and the King's Dragoon Guards. As these regiments became weaker, they were brought to the front, and several charges were made in this order—the Heavy Brigade on the left, Trip's Carabiniers in the centre, and Dornberg's German Legion cavalry on the right. An English officer, Captain Batty, of the Grenadier Guards, declared that 'he saw a Belgian cavalry regiment fight valiantly with the Cuirassiers in a manner never to be forgotten.'

This was no doubt the occasion when Trip's Carabiniers forced the Cuirassiers to retire into the hollow in the rear of La Haie Sainte, and probably this was the very charge in which General

Barnes, the English Adjutant-General, took part and received his wounds. In one of these charges, Count D'Hane, of the 2nd Carabiniers, killed a French officer in single combat. At seven in the evening, almost immediately before he was wounded, the Prince of Orange thus addressed the 2nd Carabiniers: 'Resume your position, brave Carabiniers! You have done enough for to-day,' at the same time seizing the Colonel's hand. There were loud shouts from the regiment of 'Vive le Roi! Vive notre brave Prince!' and the troopers clinked their swords together in the air.

We now come to the practical test of the killed and wounded. The 1st Carabiniers lost 3 officers killed, 25 men killed; 8 officers wounded, and 66 men wounded. The 2nd, 1 officer killed, 87 men killed; 4 officers wounded, and 64 men wounded. The 3rd, 32 men killed, 2 officers wounded, and 29 men wounded. Of the wounded officers several died, including the Colonels of the first and third regiments, Coenegracht and Lichtleitner. The 8th Croy Hussars, which is described in the records of the time as a good mixed regiment, charged several times and lost very heavily. Its death-roll numbered 1 officer killed, 132 men killed; 7 officers wounded, and 145 men wounded. When the battle began it contained 400 men, but the only remaining squadron took part in the final charge under Vandeleur. The one officer killed of this regiment was the young Count Camille du Chastel de la Howarderie. He was the second of three brothers who were present at the battle. His elder brother, Alberic, of the 2nd Carabiniers, was A.D.C. to the Prince of Orange, and his younger brother, Adolphe, was also in the 8th Hussars.

I read from the private archives of this ancient family, an ancestor of which took part in the civil wars of our Edward II., that Count Camille was struck in the breast by a cannon-ball very late in the evening, and after the regiment had made its final charge. The remains of the 5th Light Dragoons made at least two charges: the first against Jacquinot's Lancers, in conjunction with the 12th Dragoons; and the second against Kellermann's Cuirassiers, in which General Van Merlen was killed. Lieut.-General Collaert, commanding the whole cavalry division, was also wounded, and before the battle closed was obliged to resign the command of the cavalry to Trip. General Van Merlen had a presentiment that he would be killed in the battle. He wrote to this effect to his wife at Antwerp, and while breakfasting with General Collaert on the morning of the battle, he repeated it. Curiously enough, he figures among the 'missing,' because his body was never found, despite the efforts of his family to discover it.* The total cavalry losses, including missing, were 12 officers killed, 616 men killed; 38 officers wounded, and 596 men wounded—a total of 1,262, or more than a third of the number present. They also lost at Quatre Bras and Waterloo 1,630 horses.

There remains now only to describe the part taken by the third division under General Chassé, but this was the most important of all. This force was first posted at and near the village of Braine l'Alleud, where is now the nearest railway-station to the battlefield. About two o'clock, when the battle had fully developed in front, and Wellington's apprehension as to his right being turned had become less, this division was ordered to advance and support the British right under Lord Hill. About three o'clock General de Chassé reached the new position assigned him behind the Nivelles road. His first brigade (Detmer's) lined the road nearest the farm of Mont St. Jean, while the second brigade (Aubremé) lower down was placed in column formation of double battalions. The late General Mercer, who commanded a battery at Waterloo, gives in his diary the following graphic picture of the arrival of these Belgian, or, rather, Netherlands, troops on the rear of his position:

'Suddenly loud and repeated shouts, not English hurrahs, drew our attention. There we saw two dense columns of infantry pushing forward at a quick pace towards us. Crossing the fields, as if they had come from Merke Braine, everyone pronounced them French, yet still we lingered opening fire on them. Shouting, yelling and singing, on they came right for us, and being now not above 800 or 1,000 yards distant, it seemed a folly allowing them to come nearer unmolested. The commanding officer of the 14th, to end our doubts, rode forward, and endeavoured to ascertain who they were, but soon returned assuring us they were French. The order was already being given to fire, when luckily Colonel Gould, R.A., who was standing near me, recognised them as Belgians.'

For four hours General de Chassé remained in this position, having several times to form his men into squares as the French cavalry, passing through the British lines, reached his force.

* In an ode on Waterloo, published at Antwerp in 1816 by the Chevalier de Wolff, occur the following lines:

'Avec D'Aubremé, Trip, Ziethen, Kruse et Byland
Perit ce Van Merlen dont à jamais la terre
Celebrera le nom, la mort, et les hauts faits.'

Captain John Pringle described this part of the battle in the following words: 'They (Chassé's division) remained firm against the attacks of the French cavalry and repulsed it. Perhaps they even suffered more from the enemy's artillery than those in the first line, and yet at the end of the action they advanced with much firmness and regularity in order to support the first line.'

It was not, however, till seven o'clock, or a little later, that the advance of the Middle Guard, the last six battalions which the Emperor had left, except the four battalions of the Old Guard that were held in reserve until the retreat had actually begun, gave Chassé and his division their special opportunity of distinction. Wellington had seen the storm coming, and had moved up his second line to support the first. What made the attack more formidable was that the ammunition of several of the English batteries was giving out, and the Middle Guard accordingly advanced under a far less heavy artillery fire than the previous columns under Ney had experienced. General de Chassé perceived this in time, and he promptly moved up to the very front the Krahmer horse battery, under Major Van der Smissen,* commanding all the artillery of his force. At the same time, he moved forward his first brigade, under Colonel Detmers, consisting of the 2nd Dutch Line Regiment, the 35th Belgian Chasseurs, and four battalions of Dutch Militia. These troops were associated with the 30th and 73rd English regiments in repulsing that side of the Middle Guard attack, whereupon the general advance was ordered by Wellington, and the Detmers brigade charged, taking a prominent part in the final overthrow of the remaining battalions of the Old Guard already referred to. Striking evidence will be given of this a little further on, but it will be as well first to note that which is better known. Captain George Jones, in the *United Service Gazette* of 1845, bore testimony to 'the very officious and very opportune aid of Van der Smissen's battery.' Another English officer wrote: 'Major Van der Smissen literally cut lanes through the columns in our front. His guns were served most gloriously, and their grand metallic bang-bang, with the rushing showers of grape

* Van der Smissen subsequently married an English lady, Miss Graves (?), a relative of the Duke of Richmond. He rose to the rank of General, and his eldest son, also a General, commanded the Belgian contingent in Mexico in 1865.

that followed, were the most welcome sounds that ever struck my ears.'

A French officer of the Guard, on whose evidence M. Henri Houssaye lays great stress in his recent work, says that it was 'the masked battery' after the British guns were silent that repulsed their attack; but, of course, M. Houssaye should point out that this was only one section of the Middle Guard attack, the main part of which was received by Adams and Maitland. De Chassé contributed to the repulse of the left-hand section of this attack in conjunction with the brigade of Colin Halkett. Van der Smissen had three horses shot under him in this encounter, and his battery lost 27 men killed and 21 wounded. General de Chassé, in a letter to the Duke of Wellington from Roye sur les Mats, under date June 28, 1815, wrote: 'It was he who so well directed the light artillery of the third division, which in the battle of the 18th had the good fortune to attract the attention of your Excellency and of Lord Hill. At the moment when I attacked with the bayonet the French Guard, he seconded me in a manner above all expectation.' We learn from another contemporary source that Chassé formed his brigade in two close columns, harangued them, and led them to the charge in person, the men shouting, 'Vive le Roi!' and 'Vive la Patrie.'

Baron de Chassé himself describes, in the following extract from his interesting report on the battle, an incident of this advance:

'Seeing the enemy's Cuirassiers making an advance on my left, I hastened to the point threatened, and found there Captain de Haan, of the 19th Battalion of National Militia, with a few men. There was not a moment to lose, the enemy being ready to form up. I ordered him at once to profit by this favourable moment to attack them. He promptly jumped over a hedge, re-formed his peloton of about 50 men on the other side, and with a well-sustained fire carried death and confusion into the enemy's ranks. Then, profiting by the disorder, he charged them with the bayonet, and I had the supreme joy of seeing nearly 300 Cuirassiers flee before 50 men of the Netherlands army.'

The following letter from a sergeant-major in the 35th Chasseurs—Bruges battalion—published on July 6, 1815, in the Flemish local paper, the *Nieuwe Gazette van Brugge*, gives a graphic picture of the whole scene and of what followed when the combined British and Netherlands line charged down on the broken French army:

'COMPANS, 3 LEAGUES FROM MEAUX,
'July 1, 1815.

'The bloody battle of the 18th, where Napoleon commanded in person, commenced at seven in the morning, and at eight in the evening the whole French army fled in disorder. It was we Belgian Chasseurs who in the evening after seven o'clock attacked a square and pursued it to Charleroi. This square was composed of *vieilles moustaches* of the Guard. We commenced firing square against square, but that irritated us Chasseurs, and we called out for an attack with cold steel. This order we were happy enough to obtain from our General. It was then that you should have seen how that fine Guard fled at full speed. Never in my life shall I see again such a carnage. Not one of that Guard, nor of the few Cuirassiers who tried to help it, escaped. All perished by the bayonet. We only saw before and around us corpses of men and horses, guns, helmets and shakos. Napoleon thought that all the Belgians would range themselves on his side, but he very soon found that he was mistaken. We fought as if we were possessed. Our battalion had 150 killed and wounded. My captain, Guyot, was wounded in the side. Captain Dullart was slightly wounded. All we Bruges Chasseurs made a great booty out of the Imperial Guard.'

General de Chassé wrote in his official report: 'I am in the highest degree satisfied with the conduct of the whole of my division, particularly with those soldiers who were only a few months in our ranks, and whom we could only look upon as recruits. They gave the best proof that the blood of their ancestors flows strongly in their veins.' Ney, in his account, refers to the annihilation of four battalions of the Old Guard, and as some further evidence in corroboration of the Bruges sergeant-major's narrative it may be stated that the 35th Chasseurs bivouacked for the night—June 18-19—at Rossomme, the furthest point occupied by any of the troops under the orders of Wellington. Two other regiments of Chassé's division, belonging to Aubremé's brigade—viz., 3rd Dutch and 36th Chasseurs—bivouacked at La Belle Alliance. Chassé's division, according to Van Löben Sels, lost 1 officer killed (Colonel Arnauld Tilli or Van Thielen, according to another spelling, of the 6th Militia), 402 men killed and missing, 13 officers wounded, and 251 men wounded, or 667 in all. It seems that the real loss must have been greater, because Van Löben Sels, while mentioning Guyot and Roberti as the wounded officers of the 35th Chasseurs, does not put down any killed and wounded among the men of the 35th Chasseurs, which the Bruges sergeant-major estimated at 150, and which another account that I have before me gives as 70 killed alone.

With the following correspondence between General de Chassé

and Lord Hill, which English writers have studiously ignored, the part played by the third Netherlands division at Waterloo may be left to the reader's impartial judgment. The general dissatisfaction of the army at Wellington's report* of the battle has been alluded to. General de Chassé was not less dissatisfied with it than the majority of the English officers present. He gave expression to his feelings in the following letter to Lord Hill, under whose orders he served :

'BOURGET,
'*July* 5, 1815.

'YOUR EXCELLENCY,

'It was only yesterday that I read the report which H.E. the Duke of Wellington has made on the subject of the battle of the 18th ult. On that day I had the honour to serve with my division under the orders of your Excellency. As no mention is made in the report of that division, I must presume that its conduct entirely escaped the attention of your Excellency when making your report to the Duke of Wellington. I find myself under the hard necessity of stating myself to your Excellency the facts as they took place, and the part which I believe my division had in the success of the day.

'Towards evening, seeing that the fire of the artillery on the right slackened, I proceeded there to learn the cause. I was informed that ammunition was wanting. I saw very distinctly that the French Guard was advancing towards these guns; foreseeing the consequences, I caused my artillery to advance to the crest, and ordered it to keep up the liveliest fire possible. At the same time, leaving the second brigade, commanded by Major-General d'Aubremé, in reserve, and in the formation of two squares in échelon, I formed the first brigade, commanded by Colonel Detmers, in close column, and charged the French Guard. I had the happiness to see it give way before me. Through delicacy I did not make a report of this fact, being entirely persuaded that your Excellency would mention it in your report, and that with so much the more confidence that your Excellency honoured me two days after the battle (being then at Nivelles) with the expression of your contentment with the conduct of my artillery as well as with that of my infantry. But seeing my error, I should deem myself wanting in my duty towards the brave men that I had the satisfaction of commanding, and even towards the whole of my nation, if I did not make it my task to remedy this omission by begging your Excellency to be so good as to render the justice to these brave troops which I am persuaded that they deserved. They attach the greatest value to the matter, and are deeply sensible of the honour of having contributed to so glorious a victory, etc., etc.

'DE CHASSÉ.'

---

* In his report Wellington praised 'General Van Hope, commanding a brigade of infantry of the King of the Netherlands.' No General of that or any similar name was present. I think there is no doubt that Wellington meant Van Bylandt, the very officer who was accused thirty years later by Siborne of running away!

Lord Hill's reply:

'PARIS,
'*July* 11, 1815.'

'YOUR EXCELLENCY,

'I have the honour to acknowledge the receipt of your letter of the 5th inst., which only reached me yesterday.

'In the report that I had the honour to make to H.E. the Duke of Wellington on the battle of June 18, I made special mention of the conduct of your Division during that day, and I did not omit to mention that it advanced to repulse the attack of the French Imperial Guard. Unfortunately, the report of H.E. the Duke of Wellington was already sent to London before the arrival of my own report. Nevertheless, I am well assured that His Excellency is informed of the fine conduct of the troops under your orders on that glorious day, and I beg your Excellency to feel convinced that it will always afford me great pleasure to show how sensible I am of it. Accept the assurance of the high consideration with which I have the honour to be your very obedient servant,

'HILL (General).'

It may be added that Lord Hill, in his report of June 20, is said to have referred to 'the steady conduct of the third division of the troops of the Netherlands under the command of Major-General Chassé,' but the report itself has never been found. It has not been discovered either among the Wellington papers at Apsley House or the Hill papers in the British Museum. It also appears quite clear that Lord Hill could himself have known little or nothing of the Chassé charge, because at the moment of its being made he was dismounted and momentarily unconscious. Sir Digby Mackworth, cited in Sydney's 'Life of Lord Hill,' is the authority for the fact that at the very moment of the attack by the French Guard, Lord Hill's horse was shot and rolled over, severely bruising the General. It was not known what had become of him for half an hour, or until after the repulse of the French Guard.

The Duke of Wellington went to Brussels on June 19, and, not having time to write a full report for King William, requested H.E. Baron de Capellen to say to the King that it was impossible to gain a victory more complete than that of the 18th, and that he had never taken part in any battle like it; that the result remained doubtful until six o'clock; that he could not sufficiently praise the conduct of the troops, nor find eulogiums great enough for the Prince of Orange, who had so well directed the movements throughout all the day that, from the commencement to the end, he had not had any need to send him a single order.

The Duke of Wellington's letter, written from Nivelles on June 21 to the Prince of Orange, stating, 'I send you my report for the King,' and asking him to insert the name of the aide-de-camp who presented it to His Majesty, shows that on that date he did send in a report as Field-Marshal of the Netherlands. This document, which has never been published or been so much as alluded to, would set all controversy at rest, as it contains what Wellington himself wrote about the Dutch-Belgian troops under his orders. It is probable that this paper will yet be found among the archives, not of the War Department at the Hague, but of the Dutch Royal Family.

Reference has several times been made to Baron Constant de Rebecque, Chief of the Staff to the Prince of Orange. The following is the characteristic letter he wrote to his wife on June 19 from the King's anteroom at Brussels:

'Hurrah! Victoria! At last he is utterly beaten by the genius and perseverance of the Chief (Patron = Wellington). Boney was put to the rout last evening. I have received three contusions, but no blood lost except that of my pretty mare, which received first a ball in her leg, and then one in the head that killed her.'

IV

After the Battle

A few lines will suffice to sum up the events subsequent to the battle in which the Belgians had taken a prominent and honourable part. One little incident may in the first place be preserved. An officer, Lieutenant Van Uchelen, was taken prisoner by the French on the 17th, and sent to Charleroi the next day. There he was forgotten by the French, and during the night of 18th-19th he raised the townspeople, organized them into a police, and was in possession when the victors arrived on the 19th.

The treatment of the wounded of all nationalities by the inhabitants of Brussels deserves record. On June 17, when the number of wounded from Quatre Bras warned the authorities of what would follow, the Burgomaster of Brussels issued a notice that that city was to be considered the Grand Hospital of the Allied army, and he appealed for supplies of lint, old linen, mattresses and palliasses. He also notified all well-to-do people that they must provide accommodation for the wounded. On the morning of the 18th, when the cannon from Waterloo could

The Prince of Orange, while Wounded, in the Palace at Brussels.

be distinctly heard, the same functionary requested the brewers to send their waggons with barrels of water out along the Chaussée de Waterloo to meet the wounded, and thus refresh them on their way. The brewers complied, but filled their barrels with beer instead of water. Altogether 20,000 wounded were tended in Brussels. This number so far exceeded all the available accommodation that the wounded were laid out on straw under the old wall of the city, between the Louvain and Namur Gates. All these landmarks have disappeared, but the visitor to Brussels will find the line of the part of the old rampart referred to in the Avenue des Arts and the Boulevard du Regent. The Duke of Wellington wrote a personal letter to the Burgomaster, thanking him and the citizens of Brussels for their great kindness to the wounded.

The *Times* of June 30, 1815, announced that 'the brave Belgian troops who have gathered so many laurels in a few days have just been rewarded for it; it is they who precede the army which is marching to Paris.' The first division, under Prince Frederick of Orange, not having suffered at all, was pushed on at once into France. Reinforced by the light cavalry under General Ghigny, it took part in the sieges of Le Quesnoy, Peronne, Valenciennes, and Condé. At Peronne a Belgian battery sufficiently distinguished itself to obtain the thanks of Wellington, and its Colonel (De Man) died of the wounds he received on the occasion. On the close of the campaign the Netherlands troops garrisoned Picardy, and were warmly thanked by the population when leaving in 1817 for their good conduct. After Waterloo the officers and soldiers of the Belgian and Dutch armies were specially included in our Prince Regent's grant for Waterloo and Paris. On July, 17, 1817, the sums were personally distributed. It is unnecessary to go through the different grades, but each private received 61 francs 60 centimes, and a General's share was 30,589 francs. In this public and irrefutable manner the Netherlands army was declared to be worthy to share on equal terms with its British comrades in that memorable battle. From that honourable list one regiment indeed was excluded, the Cumberland Hussars of the Hanoverian army, and in the same black category also figured the 1st Company of the 4th Battalion of the British Corps of Sappers. But although these two bodies misbehaved,* no one would dare to accuse the

* In *Colburn's United Service Magazine*, April, 1855, it was stated that 'many English and Hanoverian officers and soldiers fled at Waterloo.'

armies to which they belonged of any shortcomings in courage or in conduct. The accusations have been reserved solely for the Belgians, whom Alison declared guilty because of the cowardice and flight of the German Cumberland Hussars!* *Magna est veritas et prævalebit,* and facts are sure to triumph in the end. Now that they are placed fairly before the world, the misconceptions that have too long commanded ready acceptance about the conduct of the Belgians at Quatre Bras and Waterloo must gradually pass away.

Wellington, in his despatch of August 8, 1815, wrote on this very point: 'Better to pass these parts of history in silence than to tell all the truth.'

* The result of the court-martial held at Hanover was as follows: Colonel Hake, commanding the Cumberland Hussars, was cashiered and degraded; Major Mellzing, second in command, was severely reprimanded; but 'the regiment was acquitted of having disordered the ranks of the army.'

APPENDIX

1. Report of General Chassé ⎫ relating to the Third
2. ,, ,, Lieut.-Colonel Van Delen ⎭ Division.
3. ,, ,, General de Perponcher ⎫ relating to the
4. ,, ,, Colonel Van Zuylen van Nyevelt ⎭ Second Division.
5. ,, ,, General Trip
6. ,, ,, General Ghigny ⎫ relating to the
7. ,, ,, Colonel Hoyink van Papendrecht ⎬ Cavalry.
8. ,, ,, Captain Petter ⎭
9. ,, ,, the Prince of Orange

LETTER OF LIEUTENANT-GENERAL BARON CHASSÉ TO H.R.H. THE PRINCE OF ORANGE (PRESERVED AMONG THE ARCHIVES OF THE DEPARTMENT OF WAR AT THE HAGUE).

BOURGET, *July* 4, 1815.

THE forced marches which the Third Division has made since June 18, as well as the stoppage of the postal service, are the causes that up to the present I have not had the honour to send your Royal Highness the list of officers who distinguished themselves during that glorious victory. I would not have added thereto the report of our movements and of what the Division accomplished, being persuaded that General Lord Hill (under whose command I found myself by your Royal Highness' order) had done so; but the Duke of Wellington's report makes me see very distinctly how much I have been deceived in my just expectation. I therefore took the liberty of addressing myself to Lord Hill on that account, and I have the hourr to send herewith a copy of my letter.

It is for this reason that I take the liberty of giving to your Royal Highness a report of what my Division did on that day.

The position assigned to me by Lord Hill was as follows: One battalion remained stationed at Braine la Leud, and two battalions were placed with the right wing resting on that village, and the left extending in the direction of the Second English Division. The remainder of the Division was stationed behind the village, with its left resting on the English Division just mentioned, whilst the right extended as near as possible to the wood of Soignes. Towards 3 o'clock of the afternoon, the Division received the order to move in an oblique direction towards the chaussée from Nivelles to Brussels. The brigades were formed in column, sometimes in line and sometimes in square. These manœuvres were executed with a coolness which would have done honour to veteran troops, despite a violent cannonade which caused sufficiently great ravages in the ranks.

During several hours they remained in this trying position; they confronted death with intrepidity, and when one of their comrades was hit mortally, they cried out, ' Long live the King! Long live the Fatherland!' Towards evening, as I perceived that the artillery placed in front of us on the height, if it did not absolutely cease firing, slackened very considerably, I proceeded there as quickly as possible to learn the cause, and I learnt that it was the want of ammunition. Seeing at the same moment that the French Guard was moving forward to attack this artillery, I did not hesitate an instant to order the advance on the height of our artillery commanded by Major Van der Smissen, who at once opened a violent fire.*

I ordered Major-General d'Aubremé to remain in reserve with two columns in echelon, while I advanced with the First Brigade, commanded by Colonel Detmers, in close column upon the enemy, and I had the pleasure to see the French Guard give way before the brigade. I pursued the fleeing enemy until the obscurity of the night prevented our proceeding further. I bivouacked for the night with my troops until the next day, when I received the order to march to Nivelles, where the Second Brigade rejoined me in the best order with the artillery.

I was in the highest degree satisfied with the conduct of the whole of my Division, particularly with the soldiers who had only been ten months in the ranks, and who could only be considered as recruits. They gave the best proof that the blood of their ancestors flows potently in their veins.

The two brigade commanders, Major-General D'Aubremé and Colonel Detmers, as well as Major Van der Smissen, commanding the artillery, were particularly remarked for their bravery, coolness and prudence. I add the reports of the commanders of the brigades and of the artillery in the original, in which your Royal Highness may see the details of that day. I regret that Colonel Detmers in his report does not mention the brave Colonel Speelman. He satisfied me in a special degree, and maintained his already well-merited reputation, as well as Colonel Aberson and Lieutenant-Colonel L'Honneux.

At the same time it is my duty to place under the notice of your Highness an act of excellent courage. At the moment that the Grenadiers of the Guard were attacked and repulsed by Colonel Speelman with part of the First Brigade, I saw on my left a movement made by the enemy's Cuirassiers on a height. I proceeded to the spot immediately, and found there Captain de Haan of the 19th Militia Battalion with a few soldiers. It was the moment to profit by the disorder before giving them time to form up, so I ordered him to attack the Cuirassiers at once. Followed by his soldiers, he jumped over a hedge, re-formed his platoon of about fifty men on the other side, and his brisk fire carried death and confusion into the enemy's ranks. He then profited by their disorder, and falling upon them with fixed bayonets, I had the inexpressible joy of seeing nearly 300 Cuirassiers flee before fifty Netherlanders.

* I give the following important note by Colonel F. de Bas: 'This was to meet the *second* attack of the Middle Guard. The horse battery (eight guns) of Krahmer de Bichin took up its position south of the hollow road in front of the two squares of Sir Colin Halkett. The field battery of Lux was stopped by an undulation in the ground, and did not fire.' No doubt reference is made to the steep bank alongside the Nivelles road, a sunken road, as well as that to Wavre.

Captain Gezelschap and Van Hemert of the 4th Militia Battalion also distinguished themselves much. I saw the latter, whose company is still in the best condition, act with much courage against the cavalry.

It would show a want of appreciation of your Royal Highness' well-known generous character if I were to recommend these brave officers and others to your good graces, yet I feel obliged to mention the officers of my staff as follows:

Major and Chief of the Staff Van Delen; my Adjutants, Captains de Boer and Van Omphal; Captain Beelaerts and Captain of Engineers Anemaet; also Lieutenant and Chamberlain to His Majesty, Baron Van Grovestins.

All these officers greatly distinguished themselves, and rendered me good service. I admired Baron Van Grovestins, who had never been under fire, for his coolness; the others proved that they were old soldiers.

It is nearly two months since I requested the grade of Lieutenant-Colonel for Major Van Delen, and that of Major for Captain de Boer; both are officers who have served with distinction during many years.

Lieutenant-General commanding the first* corps of the Royal Netherlands army in the field under the orders of H.R.H. Prince Frederick,

BARON CHASSÉ.

STATEMENT AS TO THE CONDUCT OF THE THIRD DIVISION OF THE ROYAL NETHERLANDS ARMY ON THE DAYS OF 15TH, 16TH, 17TH, AND 18TH, UP TO THE MORNING OF THE 19TH JUNE, 1815.

The Division named was cantoned behind Binche; its right wing was at Thieu; its left at Chapelle Harlemont; on the front it occupied Peronne, and in the rear its cantonments extended as far as Bois d'Haines and Famillereux. Fay was assigned as its rallying-point. In the morning of the 15th, it was announced that the French army had crossed the Sambre, and was advancing on Marchennes au Pont. The Division immediately made ready for battle, and marched to Fay, the rallying-point named, with the exception of two battalions which remained at Thieu and Stripy, to cover an eventual retreat on the part of the cavalry from the neighbourhood of Mons, by the defiles which lead to the places named. The Division drawn up along the road that passes through Fay remained there until six in the evening, when the General commanding received the order to advance with his Division to the heights behind La Haine, where he was to await fresh orders. The General bivouacked the Division in front of Baume, and detached two battalions with a few guns to cover the passage of the Haine to the villages of Haine St. Pierre and Haine St. Paul. In addition, patrols were sent along all the roads to carry out without ceasing fresh reconnaissances.

Early in the morning of the 16th, the General received the order to march for Nivelles with his Division. This order was executed at daybreak. At Arquennes three companies of the 12th Line Battalion were left to support the cavalry; the three other companies of that battalion were destined to

* At Waterloo Chassé commanded the third corps or division. In consequence of the wound of the Prince of Orange, his brother, Prince Frederick, was raised to the command-in-chief, and Chassé was transferred to the command of the first corps, that which had taken no part in Waterloo, but remained at Hal.

occupy Nivelles and followed the Division. When the Division reached Nivelles, it found the approaches to and streets of that place so crowded with English troops and their baggage, that it took a considerable time to traverse it.

The Division then received an order to march on Hal and to bivouack there, and this order was executed between one and two o'clock in the afternoon. In the interval we could hear in the orchards beyond the town the firing from the engagement at Quatre Bras.

During the early evening the First Brigade of this Division received orders to move to Arquennes, where it was to take the place of a brigade of English troops, while the Second Brigade remained bivouacked at the same place. The First Brigade found in the neighbourhood of that place the Netherlands cavalry and part of the Horse Artillery.

In the morning of the 17th, a battalion (the 4th) was detached from that brigade to take up a position on the road leading from Petit-reux to Nivelles. About eleven o'clock the Division was ordered to call in the detached brigade, and to march by the grand route for Waterloo. The gate leading to this road and the other issues were so crowded with the English baggage, that it was very difficult to pass along, especially for the artillery. Nevertheless, the Division reached the heights over Braine-la-leu. Whilst there commenced on our right (east) flank a fire from the enemy's skirmishers, I met here the Quartermaster-General Baron de Constant, who gave me the order to lead the Division to Braine-la-leu, and to arrange it in battle order in close columns before that place. The General commanding being in advance, I transmitted this order to the brigade commanders, who executed it, but shortly afterwards the General in command (Chassé) rejoined the Division, and after executing a reconnaissance at Braine-la-leu and in the neighbourhood, His Excellency caused the Division to advance across Braine-la-leu, and to take up another position behind that place. Towards evening this position was again changed, and the First Brigade was ordered to place itself in the town and in front of it, and to defend it with the utmost energy. In consequence the battalion of 35th Chasseurs was placed on the right, the 2nd of the Line in the centre, and the 4th Militia Battalion on the left of the town. These battalions threw out right and left as well as in front the necessary posts. They were also sufficiently under the cover of hollow roads, gardens and hedges, whilst the 6th and 19th Battalions of National Militia remained in the public square of Braine-la-leu as a reserve. Also the 17th Militia Battalion was ordered to post itself further to the left of the town, and to keep up communications with part of the English army encamped not far from there.

On the other side the Second Brigade was posted on the right behind Braine-la-leu, with its front turned obliquely towards the route from Nivelles to Brussels; the right wing a little in the rear. This brigade had in front of it marshy ground, planted with hedges and bushes. The 36th Chasseur Battalion was ordered to occupy this ground, in order to cover the brigade's front. This battalion took up its position there, and also detached a company of flankers to occupy all the thickets and outlets. This was done under the eyes of several hostile patrols. During the evening and the whole of the night rain fell in torrents, from which the troops suffered much in their bivouac. Information came to the effect that the enemy's patrols were approaching from the side of Bois Seigneur Isac, and that there was reason to fear that the enemy might partially turn our position on that side, and in that manner take us in the back. As the General had no cavalry at his disposal to follow these movements, he gave the order to the 13th Battalion of the Line to occupy a wood not far from there, and from this position the battalion named could watch the enemy. Being distant an hour's march from the main body, it still could preserve in any event a sure retreat through the Hal woods.

It was under these circumstances that day broke. Staff officers were sent to Assenberg and to Hal, to learn if provisions and ammunition could be found there in case of need. Some hostile patrols having approached our advanced posts, a few Chasseurs of the 36th Battalion were taken prisoners, and a sentry of the 12th Line Battalion was wounded. About six o'clock the General was informed by an order that H.R.H. the Prince of Orange would that day command the centre of the army, and that the Division was to await the orders it should receive either from the English General, Lord Hill or from H.E. the Marshal Duke of Wellington himself.

During the interval the General commanding caused all the necessary preparations to be made so as to be able, in case of necessity, to immediately close all the points of egress from Braine-la-leu.

At the commencement of the action, all the outlying detachments and battalions rejoined the main body. The First Brigade left the 6th Battalion of National Militia to guard the town, whilst the 17th Militia Battalion kept its first position, and while the brigade with its four other battalions advanced in front of Braine-la-leu, it approached the chaussée from Brussels, where it halted. The Second Brigade passed through the town of Braine-la-leu, and stationed itself on the left in the fields, but shortly afterwards it resumed its march to place itself on the right wing of the Second English Division. The General divided the Second Brigade into two sections of three battalions each. This brigade was then for a certain time exposed to the fire of the enemy's guns. The battalion of the First Brigade left at Braine-la-leu detached a company from its left wing and sent it to the heights on the right of that place. This battalion fired upon the enemy's cavalry.

Towards 3 o'clock in the afternoon an aide-de-camp of H.E. Marshal the Duke of Wellington brought an order for the four battalions of the First Brigade posted in advance to continue their march in line. When they reached a point within range of the fire of the enemy's artillery, another Adjutant brought them an order to form in square. After they had remained thus for a little time, the General commanding, who in the interval had caused the Second Brigade also to advance in line, gave the order for the whole of the First Brigade to assemble, and to range itself in order of battle along the chaussée to Brussels. In consequence the two detached battalions again rejoined the corps, and resumed their regular place in the order of battle. The First Brigade then found itself ranged for battle behind and along the chaussée, and on its right wing was the Second Brigade, with its sections in two columns. Both had been as much during the march as in this new position exposed to a very violent artillery and shell fire. They remained one hour in this position, until, as the evening was getting late, General Chassé perceived that the English artillery placed in front of us on the height, without completely ceasing its fire, perceptibly slackened it, and hastened to the spot to ascertain the cause. Learning that ammunition was wanting, and seeing at the same time that the French Guard was making a movement to attack the English artillery, His Excellency, without losing a moment, ordered our artillery, commanded by Major Van der Smissen, to advance up to the crest and to commence a very sustained fire. During the interval an English aide-de-camp, who moved off immediately afterwards, came to Colonel Detmers, and brought him the order to place himself in the first line with three battalions. Whereupon the said Colonel advanced by sections in column with the 35th Chasseurs, the 2nd of the Line, and the 4th Militia. He marched by the side of the heights occupied by the English army. These battalions advanced in a manner to be more or less sheltered against the musketry fire, leaving the bayonets alone exposed. Having at last found room to continue its advance to the left of two battalions ranged in battle order which were keeping up a rapid fire by files, and between a battalion placed in triangle behind the position, the battalions specified changed position towards the right and advanced in line at the moment when the battalion drawn up in triangle, as well as a corps of rifles on its left flank, commenced to recoil. By this time His Excellency had returned to the Division, and, after a pointed address, sufficiently short, but very energetic, brought up to the front the other three battalions of the First Brigade.

Leaving General D'Aubremé with the Second Brigade in reserve, His Excellency then reunited all the battalions of the First Brigade, and advanced against the enemy in close column at the head of the brigade, ordering the Charge. With shouts of 'Long live the House of Orange!' 'Long live the King!' the brigade rushed forward, despite a very heavy musketry fire, and although threatened on the flank by an attack of cavalry, when suddenly the French Guard, against whom our attack was directed, left its position and disappeared before us.

The brigade pursued the enemy until an advanced hour of the evening. The obscurity of the night and the ardour of the pursuit threw the brigade into some little disorder. One part of it, commanded by Colonel Detmers, received an order to halt about 10 o'clock at night from the Quartermaster-General, Baron de Constant de Rebecque, whilst another part, with which I found myself, and which had then arrived in close proximity to the Prussian troops, was stopped by myself. As I was looking about for a spot for a bivouac, I again met H.E. Baron Chassé, who ordered us to bivouac in the orchard of a farm near Plancenoit and here to await daybreak.

In the meanwhile the Second Brigade, after the departure of the First, had remained in its first position. It had also to sustain for some time a severe fire from artillery until the moment when an aide-de-camp from Lord Hill came to inform General D'Aubremé that the Second English Division was about to advance, and that his brigade was to follow up this movement. From this it resulted that this brigade, which had up to that only felt the fire in front, was now exposed to it on its left flank as well.

Nevertheless, the two columns of the brigade bore themselves very well, ready at any moment to form into squares. A quarter of an hour later the same Adjutant of Lord Hill came with an order for the brigade to move to the right in order to replace the Second English Division, which continued its forward march. The brigade having taken up this position, the aide-de-

APPENDIX

camp returned to General d'Aubremé with the news that the battle had clearly turned in our favour, and brought at the same time an order to this Second Brigade to advance in two lines on the right wing of the English artillery, a position in which it bivouacked for the night on the battle-field.

In the morning of the 19th the two brigades received the order to proceed to Nivelles. They reunited on the chaussée before that town, and established their bivouac at Bois Seigneur Isac.

Lieutenant-Colonel, Chief of the Staff of the Third Division,
C. VAN DELEN.

Montmorency, November 11, 1815.

REPORT OF THE SECOND DIVISION.

The incessant marches and continual bivouacking of the Division, together with the unavoidable delay in forwarding my report, have prevented me from obeying your Highness' orders to send in a list of the names of the officers who, on the 15th, 16th, and 18th of June specially distinguished themselves. I advisedly used the word 'distinguished,' as all the officers of my Divison during these glorious days thoroughly did their duty.

Without the least warning of the enemy being near, without having been advised that the day before the Prussian troops had been attacked at Thuin, the cantonment of Frasnes was unexpectedly attacked at 5 o'clock in the afternoon of the 15th of June.

The 2nd Battalion Nassau and the battery of mounted artillery which were stationed at that place immediately united, and, skirmishing, took up a position in front of Quatre Bras, from which the enemy tried in vain to dislodge them. Major van Norman, who commanded the infantry, most vigorously aided the movement of the artillery, although his left flank was seriously menaced, and he was obliged to make a stand in front of the village until all the war material had been got out of the park. The Captain of artillery, Byleveld, distinguished himself especially by the coolness with which he executed his movements and the intelligent judgment he displayed in placing his guns.

The Prince of Saxe-Weimar, who commanded my Second Brigade, having brought the remainder of his troops together at Quatre-Bras, took up an excellent strategic position in front of the village, where, after exchanging a few shots, he was left undisturbed by the enemy.

In the meantime the whole of the First Brigade, with the battery of foot artillery, had been concentrated by me at Nivelles with the intention of marching on Quatre Bras for the support of the Second Brigade, as I had been informed by some deserters and Prussians in flight that Charleroi had been evacuated, and the whole of the Prussian army had been removed to Wavre. I considered that the position at Quatre Bras, which was now unprotected, ought to be strengthened, and that whilst awaiting there orders and reinforcements everything possible should be done to prevent the enemy from marching upon Brussels.

At 2 o'clock of the morning of the 16th I marched, with the 27th Battalion of Chasseurs and the 8th Battalion of Militia, to Quatre Bras, in order to strengthen this point and take over the command of the troops. Not knowing whether the enemy had also made an attack on Binche, in which case the entire front of my right wing would have been exposed, I left Major-General van Bylandt with the three other battalions of his brigade and the battery of foot artillery at Nivelles, with instructions to defend that point as long as possible, and at the last extremity to retire to Mont St. Jean, and to take up his position at the point where the chaussées of Nivelles and Quatre Bras meet, and to maintain himself there until I joined him with the Second Brigade.

Immediately outside Nivelles I fell in with a detachment of fifty horse of the 2nd Silesian Regiment of Hussars, which had been cut off from the Prussian troops. Being without cavalry, I proposed to First-Lieutenant Zehelin, who was in command of that detachment, to accompany me to Quatre Bras. This young officer hesitated not an instant, and your Royal Highness himself has witnessed his courage and discernment.

On my arrival at Quatre Bras, I found that the Prince of Saxe-Weimar had made the best possible arrangements. I somewhat extended the lines and reinforced the posts in the wood, which was the key of the position.

Your Royal Highness having himself come later on to Quatre Bras and taken over the command of my Division, I shall refrain from entering into details as to the conduct of my troops on that day. Your Royal Highness himself led the beautiful charge of the 5th Battalion of the Militia. Your Royal Highness has been an eye-witness to the sang-froid with which a few companies of Nassau Chasseurs repulsed the attack of the French cavalry, and your Royal Highness has himself observed the undaunted bravery displayed by the 27th Battalion of Chasseurs and the men of the Second Brigade, who succeeded in holding the wood against the repeated attacks of the Imperial Guard.

The battery of foot artillery which had been placed in position in the best order by Major van Opstall was almost entirely destroyed by a charge of cavalry. Lieutenant Winssinger, who was left with two guns on that day, performed his duty in the most exemplary manner.

Your Royal Highness having on the 18th assigned to the Division its several positions, I shall not here repeat the arrangements of the troops.

The First Brigade, which was placed in the centre, was exposed to the fiercest attacks of the enemy; the several corps vied with each other in bravery; and I should consider myself failing in my duty if I neglected to bring their superior officers under your Highness' notice. The Lieutenant-Colonels Westenberg, Grünenbosch, Van den Sanden, Singendonck and De Jongh, worked their several battalions so well together, that they were enabled to keep the enemy at bay until the whole brigade was disposed in battle array against the overwhelming force of the enemy. In this engagement the brigade suffered much; Major-General van Bylandt was wounded, as also the superior officers of all the battalions; the officers who took their places all behaved splendidly, especially the Captain-Major of the brigade, Van Zuylen van Nyevelt, who displayed the greatest activity, and who, when his horse had been killed under him, continued his command on foot.

The Prince of Saxe-Weimar, placed on the left wing near the Castle of Frichermont, with his troops repulsed several attacks made on the position which your Royal Highness had assigned to the Second Brigade, with the result that communication with the Prussian army remained intact and the road open, from which it was intended to attack the right wing of the enemy.

APPENDIX 49

The Prince of Saxe-Weimar has given great praise to the superior officers of the several corps of the Second Brigade, and I take the liberty of calling your Royal Highness' attention among the names placed on the list to that of the Major of the regiment, Orange Nassau, Vigilius, and the Brigade-Major of the Second Brigade, van Coustoll.

Before closing this report, I think it my duty to mention to your Royal Highness the splendid behaviour of all the officers of my general staff. Colonel van Zuylen van Nyevelt, although wounded, refused to leave the battlefield, and during the three days his great military talents and tact have been of the utmost service to me. Both my adjutants, Major van de Poll, an old soldier of great military intelligence and experience, whose horse was shot dead under him, and the Captain of the volunteers, De Smeth van Deurne, who, under the fiercest cannonade, displayed the coolness of an old soldier, have been most useful to me in transmitting my orders. The Major of the general staff, Taets van Amerongen, when two horses had been shot dead under me, gave me his and continued his service on foot.

On this day, so auspicious for the Netherlands troops, in which, by the blood shed, the ancient glory of our arms has been revived, I particularly deplore the loss of the First Lieutenant of the general staff, Van Haeren, a young man who had joined the army as a volunteer and gave the fairest promise; he was struck by a cannon-ball whilst in the act of executing a manœuvre.

Among the seriously wounded and killed of the ninety officers which the Division lost in the three days of the 15th, 16th and 18th of June, were several officers of great merit, whose deaths are an immense loss to His Majesty's army.

I enclose a list of names of the officers who have particularly distinguished themselves, to which I refer.

The Lieutenant-General.
H. DE PERPONCHER.

Paris, July 11, 1815.

REPORT ON THE OPERATIONS OF THE SECOND DIVISION BY COLONEL VAN ZUYLEN VAN NYEVELT.

During the whole of the morning (15th June) the roar of the cannon had been heard; but as it was not usual among the several armies to give notice of the firing during practice, no heed was paid to it.

For some time past it had been the custom for the separate battalions to assemble during the day on the common drill-ground, and to retire at night to their separate quarters. In this way the troops were assembled in the afternoon of the 15th, when about four o'clock General Perponcher received intelligence from the commander of the 2nd Battalion Nassau that the firing which had been heard close to Gosselies was rapidly approaching, and that the discharges from the firearms were already distinctly visible.

His Excellency gave at once the order that the Division should be concentrated at the two alarm posts of Nivelles and Quatre Bras. But the order for the concentration at Quatre Bras had not yet reached that place when a body of Tirailleurs of the French Imperial Guard attacked the village of Frasnes where the mounted artillery and half a battalion of the Nassauers were stationed. The sound of the frequent and close firing had induced Major Normann, of the 2nd Battalion of the 2nd Nassau Regiment, to keep his men under arms and place a few outposts. About five o'clock, after things had been quiet for about an hour, the latter were suddenly surprised at the onset of a body of French cavalry. The first flank company, under Captain Müller, and eighty volunteers under Lieutenant Hoelschen, were sent against the enemy and kept them at bay.

A general order had been previously given to Major Normann that in case of alarm he should concentrate his battalion at Frasnes, and on no account abandon the artillery, for which he would be personally held responsible; but when he saw the enemy come in large numbers out of the wood as well as from the direction of Gosselies, and considering that the artillery, when moving out of the park, had to pass in front of the village, whilst in order to join his brigade at Quatre Bras his left flank would be for half an hour exposed to the enemy, and that very probably he would be cut off, he gave the order to fall back.

As soon as the enemy became aware of the movement, they made a charge, but through the foresight of Captain Bylevelt, the men from the park were already coming to the rescue, and whilst the reserves were drawing near, Major Normann placed his forces to the best advantage, stationing the artillery to the right of the road under cover of four companies, and placing the remaining companies so as to protect his flanks. The enemy, who had been for a short time kept at bay by a heavy volley of cannon and rifle fire, now pressed in superior numbers on his left flank, which determined Major Normann to take up a definite position near the farm on the highroad of Charleroi, with his front turned to Quatre Bras, and to place at the same time a strong force in the wood of Boussu. These movements were executed under a heavy fire of the enemy, but after a short engagement of the rifles and a few cannon-balls judiciously thrown among the cavalry of the enemy, the latter desisted from further harassing our position.

After the order for the concentration of the troops had been received, the Second Brigade, under Colonel the Prince of Saxe-Weimar, was stationed on the chaussée, with its front towards Gosselies; the 1st Battalion Nassau took its stand along the road from Hautain Leval, two of its companies being placed on the right edge of the wood, whilst two companies of the 3rd Battalion Nassau and the company of Grenadiers, together with two companies of the 2nd Battalion Regiment No. 28, were sent to reinforce the 2nd Battalion; the volunteer company of Chasseurs, formed in four bodies, was told off to cover the wood.

Two of the guns, with some troops, were placed somewhat in advance on the chaussée of Namur, and a 6-pounder stationed near the outpost on the Charleroi road.

At seven o'clock the Adjutant of the Second Brigade came to report to General Perponcher that the troops at Frasnes had been attacked, and that on this account the place had been evacuated by us, informing him of the position taken up by the troops.

His Excellency gave order that the position at Quatre Bras should be held as long as possible. Whilst intelligence of this event was being conveyed to the Prince of Orange and his commands requested, His Excellency dispatched to Waterloo all the superfluous artillery stores, the heavy baggage of the Division, the court-martial, the clothing depot of the camp, the staff and equipment of the hospital, and everything which could impede the movements of the army, there to await further orders.

The First Brigade and the artillery had now been brought together around Nivelles; the 27th Battalion of Chasseurs was placed in reserve on the St. Paul market-place, where, later on, they were relieved by the 7th Battalion of the Line. Until this time no reliable intelligence had been received as to the enemy's movements. We had no idea that the whole of the French army was approaching, nor of the result of the engagement near Charleroi and Gosselies, which caused the Prussians to retreat to Fleurus, and thus the whole of our left flank was left uncovered, and also the highroad to Brussels viâ Waterloo open to the enemy.

The only news that came to us as to the doings of the enemy were confused rumours, told by Prussian fugitives escaped from Thuin and Lobbes, until the arrival at the headquarters of the Division of a French assistant-captain, who, returning to his lawful allegiance, had deserted from the French army in peasant's clothes, and reported the result of the engagement with the Prussians, informing us that Buonaparte was marching with 150,000 men on Brussels.

At nine o'clock the Prince of Saxe-Weimar sent word that the enemy was very numerous, and that he feared he was not strong enough to resist an attack.

General Perponcher, in reply, commanded him to defend the position at Quatre Bras as long as possible, and should the enemy attack him in very superior numbers, to withdraw to Mont St. Jean, where in that case he would be joined by the First Brigade. At the same time His Excellency informed him that it was his intention to march that very night with two battalions to Quatre Bras, and to take over the command of that post, the General not daring to withdraw troops from Nivelles without being assured beforehand that the enemy had not made an attack on Binche, and that the Division could be replaced by the third.

In the meantime a company of Chasseurs and a company of infantry were told off to line the road between Quatre Bras and Nivelles, whilst the battalions placed outside the gates of the town, by continual rounds, made sure against a surprise of the enemy. At half-past ten an order was received from the Prince of Orange to concentrate the whole of the Division at Nivelles, where it would be supported by the Third Division, whilst the cavalry was ordered to be drawn together on the high ground of Haine St. Pierre. Although this order of not exposing the troops against the enemy in small bodies, but to oppose them in a mass, showed much prudence, General Perponcher imagined that His Royal Highness, who at the time of sending the order was in Brussels, might not have been as well informed of the movements of the French and Prussian armies as himself, and that probably His Royal Highness was in ignorance of the fact that Charleroi had been evacuated, and that the Prussians were rallying at Fleurus. His Excellency the General having from different sources obtained sure information as to the true state of affairs, and considering that it was of the highest importance that Brussels should remain protected, so as to fill the gap between himself and the Prussians, and prevent the enemy from penetrating to the defile of the Bois de Soignes, where he would be able to cut off all assistance, thought it right not to obey this command, but at all hazards to maintain the position at Quatre Bras, the order for which he renewed, and informed His Royal Highness of his decision. At 12 o'clock an officer of the General Staff arrived with a despatch from the Quartermaster-General, informing His Excellency that His Royal Highness had been advised of the movements of the enemy, and that he might be expected every minute from Brussels. The troops remained in their camps and passed the night (June 16) undisturbed. At two o'clock in the morning His Excellency started with the 27th Battalion Chasseurs and the 8th Battalion National Militia for Quatre Bras. Immediately outside Nivelles His Excellency met a detachment of fifty Prussian Hussars of the 2nd Silesian Regiment, strayed from their corps. The General, having no cavalry, proposed to Lieutenant Zehelin, who was in command of the detachment, to join his troops, which proposal the officer joyfully accepted.

On the march to Quatre Bras General Perponcher singled out the draft companies of the two battalions, and with them reached Quatre Bras at half-past two; the remainder of the troops arrived there about four o'clock.

His Excellency at once inspected the military dispositions, and found that the Prince of Saxe-Weimar had made very good arrangements; however, he extended our lines somewhat farther in order to hide our weakness from the enemy, and to strengthen the posts at the wood of Boussu.

At five o'clock the 27th Battalion of Chasseurs was placed in the first line to the left of the Charleroi road, and both the flank companies of this battalion, relieving the 3rd Battalion Nassau, were distributed over its left wing, where they were able to watch the movements of the enemy. The 8th Battalion National Militia remained in reserve in the centre of the Second Brigade behind the houses of Quatre Bras. The 2nd Battalion Nassau having sent out its scouts, soon followed by all the men of the battalion, fell in with a few cavalry patrols of the enemy and some pickets, who retired after a few shots had been exchanged. This battalion took up its stand on the high ground in the rear of Frasnes, one company guarding the village, two others holding the edge of the wood. By this movement the battalion commanded nearly the whole of the wood of Boussu, and recovered almost all the ground lost on the previous day.

In the course of reconnoitring, the detachment of Prussian Hussars made a few splendid charges on the cavalry of the enemy, whom they forced to retreat, themselves losing four men and thirteen horses. This detachment having soon after heard of the whereabouts of its own army corps, left the Division and went to Sombref. In the meantime, General Perponcher, loth to denude Nivelles entirely, had left there General Bylandt with three battalions and a battery of foot artillery; but H.R.H. the Prince of Orange, passing Nivelles at six o'clock, ordered that two battalions of the First Brigade and the Artillery should move to Quatre Bras, whilst the 7th Battalion of the Line was to remain in Nivelles until relieved by a battalion of the Third Division.

At six o'clock two companies of the left wing, which was lined by the 27th Battalion Chasseurs, were told off to seize a height, from which the enemy could watch our movements. They succeeded in taking the position, but the enemy having been reinforced by some bodies of infantry, a heavy fire from two sides prevented our men from following up their advantage. At several points little skirmishes took place, the artillery sending from time to time a volley to keep off the enemy until H.R.H. the Prince of Orange, having arrived on the battle-ground, ordered more troops to advance in a line parallel with the Charleroi road, extending the line so far that our right wing reached to within a short quarter of an hour from Frasnes, and to the edge of the wood of Boussu. The eight guns of the mounted artillery were placed in reserve in the hollows of the ground to protect them from the fire of the enemy.

Whilst the 5th and 7th Battalions National Militia with the battery of foot artillery were on their way from Nivelles to Quatre Bras, there appeared on their right flank, near Hautain Leval, in the direction of Rêves, a body of the enemy's cavalry. The commanding officer ordered the 7th Battalion to halt in front of the forest of Hailey, until the whole party should have passed; they arrived safely about nine o'clock at Quatre Bras, and were placed in reserve on the chaussée.

At seven o'clock the enemy began to reconnoitre our position by making a few cavalry charges, which were, however, repulsed with loss on his side. After things had remained quiet for over an hour, H.R.H. the Prince of Orange ordered that the soldiers should rest and that meals should be prepared in the camp.

Up to now the enemy had not appeared in great strength; the troops against whom we had had to fight consisted, besides part of the Infantry of the Line, of Chasseurs of the Guard, Lancers and mounted artillery of the Guard, belonging to the army corps of General Reille. It was quite possible that larger bodies of troops of the enemy were hidden by the Forest of Villers-Perwin and the avenues of Gosselies, behind Frasnes. However, it might easily be inferred from the movements of the enemy that the feint on Quatre Bras was intended to mask another movement, and that the attacks would not go beyond a few serious reconnoitring skirmishes; at the same time the heavy firing in the direction of Sombref gave rise to the supposition of an attack on the Prussians, who were retreating that way—the more so as it was not to be supposed that Napoleon would be strong enough to engage a separate battle on each of the two wings of his army.

Whilst on our side we were fully alive to the grave mistake that had been made in placing the boundary between the combined English and Prussian troops along the line which the enemy might choose as most favourable for his operations, should he contemplate the invasion of Belgium and take the offensive (there being in that part not a single fortress which would hinder him from invading the Southern Netherlands), it was a matter of surprise why Napoleon, after having gained already such great advantages on the Prussians, did not strain every effort to obtain possession of Quatre Bras. With this object he could have detached one or two divisions from his left wing by a similar movement, and penetrated to Brussels by way of Nivelles. He could then have seized the position at Quatre Bras by a turning movement and been at Mont St. Jean before or at the same time as our troops; and by securing the important defile of the Forest of Soignes, he would have deprived the allies of their vantage ground and prevented them from engaging on the favourable plain of Waterloo, in the battle by which, two days later, the fate of France was decided.

His Excellency the Duke of Wellington arrived at nine o'clock. After having inspected the positions, in which he altered nothing, and collected some information, he left in the direction of Sombref to find out what was taking place there.

The 2nd Battalion Nassau having been exposed to fire since the previous day, was at twelve o'clock relieved by the 3rd Battalion and sent to Quatre Bras to rest and have its meal.

Whilst these incidents were taking place, the Third Division had reached Nivelles and there relieved the battalion of our Division which had been left for the protection of the town. This battalion arrived at twelve o'clock at Quatre Bras and was formed in a compact column behind the wood. Thus the whole of the Division was brought together at Quatre Bras, in front of and in the forest of Boussu, occupying the plain of Frasnes, the left wing being placed on the chaussée of Charleroi and guarding the forest of Villers-Perwin.

The artillery was placed as follows : Two 6-pounders and a howitzer of the mounted artillery on the road to Frasnes ; one 6-pounder and one howitzer on the right side of that road ; and the other three 6-pounders of the battery on the road to Namur. The two howitzers and four of the 6-pounders of the foot battery were placed in front of the position at Quatre Bras, close to the troops of the Second Line ; Lieutenant Winsinger, with two 6-pounders, supported the right wing of the First Line ; the remainder of the artillery, with the reserve matériel, was placed behind Quatre Bras with the reserve.

From the reports of an Adjutant-General who had deserted, and of officers and soldiers whom we had made prisoners, we gained the sure information that eight divisions of infantry and four divisions of cavalry were marching against us under command of Marshal Ney, being thus divided: The first corps infantry under General Count d'Erlon, the second corps under General Reille ; two divisions of heavy cavalry under General Kellerman ; one division of light cavalry under General Piré, and one division cavalry of the Guards, the Red Lancers of which were commanded by General Colbert, and the mounted Chasseurs by General le Febvre Desnouettes.

About one o'clock the movements of the enemy became more decided ; the preliminaries distinctly proved that his object was to march on Brussels by way of Quatre Bras.

Two other companies of the 27th Battalion Chasseurs were placed farther to the left, and a number of sharpshooters (Tirailleurs) along the wood of Villers-Perwin in order to watch the movements of the enemy, whilst another company was told off for covering the foot battery most in front.

In the meantime large bodies of the enemy had come in sight, the Tirailleurs keeping up a well-sustained fire all along the line, in order to mask an important movement of their left flank towards their right.

About two o'clock the 7th Battalion of the Line was also placed in compact column on the plain, but soon afterwards it received the order to take up a position first behind the wood, afterwards to the right of it. The 7th Battalion of Militia followed on their traces and crossed the wood, which the enemy was then already attacking in force. At the same time the 5th Battalion National Militia was ordered to take its stand somewhat more to the left on the chaussée of Charleroi, and to guard a farm situated alongside that road.

APPENDIX

The 1st Battalion of the 28th Regiment and the 8th Battalion of National Militia formed the extreme of the right wing, and were placed in battle array, but soon received the order to retire and to take up their position opposite and in the rear of the wood of Boussu.

The 1st Battalion Nassau Usingen was placed in battle array in front of the forest; the companies of Captains Werneck and Trittler were placed *en tirailleurs*. They were several times charged by the Lancers of the Guard; but, led by His Royal Highness himself, they bravely repulsed these attacks. However, as the enemy was pressing forward in increasing numbers, too large to make it safe for the battalion to remain on the open ground, they received the order to withdraw to the edge of the forest of Boussu; the eight guns of the mounted artillery and two of the 6-pounders of the foot artillery took their stand near the troops of the first line and the other guns of the foot battery near those of the second line.

In this position the Division had been entirely by itself and without cavalry, all the time exposed to a heavy artillery and rifle fire, with alternate cavalry charges. We were losing already a great many men, when, towards half-past two, the enemy, with a shout of " Hurrah for the Emperor!" (" Vive l'Empereur!"), simultaneously charged our line on several points at once. We were expecting at every moment our cavalry, which did arrive soon after, but the reinforcements of the English, Scotch, and Brunswick troops, who had only been moved up from Brussels during the night of the 15th to the 16th, could not be expected for some time.

The enemy, under a heavy fire, forced our troops to abandon their position in front of the wood, and succeeded in taking possession of the greater part of it.

In falling back some of the troops took up their stand on the north side of the wood, whilst others crossed the road and arranged themselves on the most commanding part of the high ground to its left.

As the enemy was pressing on our left wing in an oblique line from the forest of Villers-Perwin, the 27th Battalion Chasseurs was moved forwards about 100 steps, in order to cover the left wing of the 5th Battalion National Militia. The companies which had been told off were attacked and repulsed before they had had time to form their ranks, and rallied themselves in the rear of the battalion. The enemy took advantage of his success to place a battery exactly in front of this battalion, which move forced it to retire. It did so, executing the movements in small bodies with the regulation distances, so as to be able at any time to form into square.

The enemy, having repulsed the 7th Battalion of the Line, made rapid progress through the wood, from which the 8th Battalion National Militia had been driven by a heavy artillery fire. The 1st Battalion of Regiment No. 28 and the 7th Battalion National Militia were still held in reserve to the right of the wood, whilst the two battalions which had been driven back again formed their ranks on the high ground in the rear of it. His Royal Highness ordered also the 2nd Battalion Nassau to advance, flanked by the 2nd Battalion of Regiment No. 28; but the enemy, by superior numbers, a well-sustained artillery and rifle fire, and uninterrupted cavalry charges, drove back the troops of the first line.

They retreated without hurry and in the best possible order, headed by the Prince of Orange and General Perponcher, whilst on both sides a heavy fire was being kept up. These troops, with both the 6-pounders of the foot battery, for the greater part made their way in an oblique line through the wood, and so reached the chaussée of Hautain Leval.

The 27th Battalion Chasseurs, who had not yet had time to close their ranks, were charged by the Red Lancers of the Imperial Guard and the 6th Regiment of Mounted Chasseurs, who broke through their lines. On this occasion this battalion lost a considerable number in wounded and prisoners; the greater part of the latter, however, managed to return to us during the night.

The enemy having thus gained possession of the greater part of the ground in front of the position, now made strenuous efforts to force the centre and to gain Quatre Bras by way of the farmhouse.

The brigade of light cavalry of General van Merlen had now arrived and had taken up its position to the left of the highroad. The vanguard of the English Division, under General Picton, and of the Brunswick troops, under the Duke of that name, arrived about three o'clock on the spot, and were stationed so as to cover our left wing, which was thus extended far along the chaussée of Sombref.

As soon as the enemy became aware that we had received reinforcements, he redoubled his attacks on the farmhouse, which was defended by the 5th Battalion National Militia. His Royal Highness personally held the command here, and, waving his hat, he rode in advance of the troops, and directed several charges on the enemy, repulsing them with heavy losses. Each time the artillery advanced a few hundred steps, and immediately had their guns pointed; but they could not long withstand the firing of the enemy's guns, which were far superior in size and number. The Captain of the foot battery was killed, several officers killed or wounded, and the horses so rapidly shot down that it was scarcely possible to keep the guns moving.

The example of His Royal Highness, followed by the Staff of the Division, so inspired the 5th Battalion National Militia, which was under the command of Lieutenant-Colonel Westenbergh, that they did miracles of bravery; but one attack had scarcely been repulsed ere the enemy made another with fresh men and in larger numbers. The light cavalry were then ordered to charge the enemy, but, carried away by their impetuosity, they rushed too far forward and fell upon the 8th and 11th Regiments of Cuirassiers, who, being far superior in numbers and arms, routed them completely with heavy loss. The Cuirassiers came now in large numbers over the roads, carrying with them some of the artillery and infantry; but when they had advanced so far as the houses of Quatre Bras, they were met by the fire of the rallying troops, who had here been brought to a stand. The First Brigade, which was placed to the right of the road, attacked the enemy's left flank, and the Second Brigade, stationed with a regiment of Scotchmen on the left side of the road, so effectually harassed his right flank by a well-sustained fire that he was forced to retreat, and in his flight had to sustain a heavy fire of the artillery, by which many were killed.

In the meantime the enemy had seized the wood. His Royal Highness ordered the 2nd Battalion Nassau, together with a few Brunswick Chasseurs, to regain possession of it. They manfully undertook the task, but the enemy being far too strong, our troops had to retire.

APPENDIX 57

The Scotch and English troops on our left wing had now advanced on the right flank of the enemy, and our troops having been rallied, an attempt was made to dislodge the enemy from the farmhouse, of which they were still in possession.

At the same time His Royal Highness ordered Colonel van Zuylen van Nyevelt, Chief of the Staff, to try with three battalions to regain possession of the part of the wood extending to the place where the 2nd Battalion Nassau had been stationed in the morning. The 7th Battalion National Militia remained in reserve; the 1st Battalion of Regiment No. 28 formed the echelons of the movement; the whole of the 2nd Battalion Nassau, with its Colonel, made its way through the wood *en tirailleurs*, and after a sharp fire drove the French Guard, who occupied it with a strong force, back as far as the point to which the order referred.

By the successful attacks on the farmhouse and on the wood we regained a large number of our wounded and prisoners, whilst the enemy only succeeded in carrying off one howitzer and two 6-pounders, which we recovered two days later.

Besides the English Division of General Picton and the Brunswick troops, both the Divisions of the Guards and of General Alten, the 1st Regiment Nassau Usingen, as well as regiments of cavalry and a large amount of artillery, had now arrived on the battlefield. The Division was therefore relieved. They were only left in charge of guarding that part of the forest which they had regained, and keeping under observation the lines of communication to the right of the forest of Boussu and the avenues on the road of Hautain Leval. A few more demonstrations of the enemy, the sending of the 1st Corps against the Prussians, and the darkness, made an end to the fighting, and both armies remained in the same positions as at the termination of the battle.

The Division encamped on the high ground in the rear of the wood of Boussu; the 1st Battalion Regiment No. 28 and the Regiment Nassau to the right of the forest, formed in column; the remainder of the troops in two lines of battle array, having on their right a Division of English, and on their left the Brunswick troops. The 5th Battalion National Militia, which had suffered most, and the 8th Battalion National Militia encamped with the artillery behind these troops, the artillery having to repair its damage. The 27th Battalion Chasseurs had been commanded by His Royal Highness himself to withdraw to Nivelles, and there spent the night.

This day had been a glorious one for the Netherlands troops. The Second Division, which was only 7,000 men strong, had alone for several hours beaten off the charges of the left wing of the enemy, who, with the whole of the 2nd Corps (which was composed of the pick of the infantry, the best cavalry, and the artillery of the Guard), strained every effort to render itself master of Quatre Bras.

The excellent dispositions taken by the Prince of Orange, in extending the troops over a long line, and placing them at so many different points, were fortunately aided by the conformation of the ground: the forest of Boussu masked all our movements, and the soldiers who occupied it made the enemy believe that we were very strong, and that the troops of which he caught sight (and which were the whole of our forces) were only the vanguards of several army corps.

But the Division could not by itself have kept the enemy much longer at bay; the men who had been the whole day exposed to the fire were very exhausted, and the great losses sustained by several of the corps made it necessary that they should have a rest ; whilst the artillery, having had three of its guns taken and four damaged, several of its ammunition waggons blown up, and most of its officers and men killed or wounded, had become almost useless.

The firing on the left wing continued till darkness had set in, and judging from the sound, it seemed as if neither of the two armies were making any perceptible progress.

June 17.—All remained calm during the night. At break of day the 27th Battalion Chasseurs returned from Nivelles, and all the corps were gathered together, with the exception of the artillery, which, having still much to do in repairing their gear, remained in the rear of our left wing under protection of the 5th Battalion National Militia. Cartridges were being distributed and the flints renewed, and as the night had been damp, the men were told to clean their arms. No other movement was observed along the line than that of a few English battalions and batteries of artillery who were filling up their ranks. A few regiments of English cavalry were placed on the right wing to keep the place of Hautain Leval under observation. Up till this time everything had been quiet, and judging from appearances, it seemed as if we should make the first attack, or at least await the enemy on the ground we occupied; but soon the news spread in the camp that the Prussians had suffered a severe defeat at Ligny, and were in full retreat upon Wavre, in order to fall back upon their reserve. We clearly saw that the Duke of Wellington, not being strong enough to withstand the whole of the French army, would be obliged to follow their retreat in order to unite again with the Prussians, and the troops were ordered to have their breakfast as fast as possible. A little later, at about nine o'clock, the Prince of Orange came to order the retreat. He himself formed the Division in bodies (pelotons) in compact columns, and rode at their head on their march towards Brussels. Close to La Caragne the corps which had been detached again joined the Division, and the troops continued their march to Genappe, preceded by the Third English Division. As the whole of the baggage of the army was being taken over the same route, they fell in on the narrow road and bridge of Genappe with the convoy of artillery and provisions which were on their way to the army; this caused an obstruction. In order to avoid confusion, the General of the Division gave order to search for a fordable spot on the left side of the town of Genappe ; this having been found, the Division crossed in double squads the arm of the Dyle which passes through Genappe, and having reached the opposite side of the town, they formed themselves on the highroad again into columns as before.

The Division had received the order to camp on, and parallel to, the highroad leading from Brussels to Nivelles, its left wing resting on the village of Mont St. Jean, the right wing extending to Braine l'Alleud ; on this understanding it would be joined by the Third Division.

Towards mid-day it began to rain ; considerable progress had already been made in the fixing of tents, when at six o'clock the order came to break up the camp and for the Division to take its stand at the extreme end of the left wing of the first line of the army; this having been accomplished, the Division camped in the very position in which it gave battle. In pursuance with this order, the Division formed itself in several sections into a column, marched with its left wing in front as far as the farmhouse of La Haye Sainte, which was approached from the left, then passed at the back of it, and swaying round to the right, fell into the line of battle on the slope of the hill of Mont St. Jean, its right wing displayed on the highroad towards Brussels and its left towards Wavre, having the low-lying road leading from the latter to Braine l'Alleud in its rear. Six cannons were distributed over the right wing to command the road to Genappe, and the three other guns placed near the left wing, on the heights overlooking the villages of Frichermont and Smohain, whilst 400 Tirailleurs were stationed from 150 to 200 paces in advance.

The Division took its position on the slope of the hill of Mont St. Jean; the ground on which stood the right wing was marshy, that occupied by the left wing heavy clay, both soaked by the rain; in the rear of the front extended the low-lying road leading from Ohain to Braine l'Alleud, lined on both sides with sallows and hawthorn hedges, where the English and Scottish Division had been posted, well protected by several 9-pounders. Facing the front lay a boggy ravine and beyond this the hills extending on both sides of Mont St. Jean. The right wing faced the farm of La Haye Sainte, and the left wing the village of Smohain, having on its left a low-lying road leading to a hill on which stood the castle of Frichermont (belonging to Mr. Beaulieu), about two musket-shots distant from the last-named village.

During these dispositions the English cavalry was being repulsed and broke through our lines, with the enemy in close pursuit. The firing of the artillery was steadily coming nearer, and the flash of the small arms could already distinctly be seen; but as the English rearguard had made a stand in front of La Haye Sainte and darkness intervened, the enemy stopped his pursuit and camped part of his troops on the hills in face of us; the row of Tirailleurs was twice relieved before nightfall.

It was a terrible night; rain fell incessantly in torrents; a cold east wind was blowing at the same time, which made the position of the soldiers, who had no straw to make tents with, nor wood to make a fire, and whe were standing ankle-deep in the water, most distressing.

June 18.—About two o'clock a.m. a false alarm brought the whole of the Division under arms; the men remained on the alert until we were quite certain that nothing had happened. Through this incident the men, who had been able to find some shelter against the rain, were also thoroughly drenched. At break of day all the troops were under arms; a few scouts of the enemy were noticed on the heights facing us, but no large bodies of soldiers were visible. During the night but few fires had been seen, perhaps owing to the heavy rain, or to the fact that the enemy had left the bulk of his army at Genappe.

At six o'clock the Brigade-Major Coustoll went with a party to reconnoitre Smohain and Frichermont, where four companies of the 1st Battalion of Regiment No. 28 were placed. At eight o'clock His Royal Highness himself inspected the line, and in his kind foresight ordered rations to be distributed.

Cartridges and flints were dealt out, and the arms got ready for emergency.

At nine o'clock His Royal Highness ordered 800 men of the Division to be despatched to strengthen the right wing, for which the 1st Battalion of the 2nd Regiment Light Infantry Nassau was told off. This battalion, under command of Captain Buschen, took possession of the farmhouse of Hougoumont, situated between the roads of Nivelles and Genappe leading to Waterloo, and by this proceeding covered the front of the right wing of the army. This farmhouse was a large building, standing in the midst of a large-sized garden, enclosed by a wall, in which loopholes were made, as also in the windows and doors.

Just in front of the farmhouse was a small copse, terminating on the road of Nivelles; three of the companies were placed in this copse, the three others entrenching themselves in the garden and in the house as well as the short time left at their disposal before the expected assault would allow.

The weather was now somewhat improving, and an hour later was tolerably dry, whilst afterwards alternate rain and sunshine continued for the whole day.

Buonaparte, having noticed that the whole of our army was in battle array and offered fight, now gave order for his troops to concentrate. This movement began to be executed at ten o'clock on the hills facing us.

At eleven o'clock some movements in the lines of the enemy seemed to indicate that they were strengthening their right wing, several cannons being moved in that direction, whilst large bodies of men were being drawn together on the hills, as if an attack on our left wing was intended.

At twelve o'clock the whole of the First Brigade and the artillery of the right wing moved farther back, in order not to hinder the evolutions of the English guns placed in their rear, and also to be less exposed to the fire of the enemy. Crossing the sunken road, the corps formed itself on the northern side of the road in the same battle array as before, supported on the right and left by the English and Scottish troops, the guns in a line with those of the English. Order was given to the 5th Battalion National Militia to remain in reserve, and to place itself in the second line, which was composed of English and Scottish troops.*

The position of the Second Brigade was as follows: The 2nd Battalion Regiment No. 28 formed in square; four companies of the 3rd Battalion Nassau *en colonne*, both behind the village and *en réserve;* the remainder of the troops were posted behind the hedges and other sheltered parts of the ground in the direction of Smouken; four companies of the 1st Battalion Regiment No. 28 occupied the castle of Frichermont, and a company of the 2nd Battalion of that regiment guarded the low-lying road of Smouken leading to the castle of Mr. Beaulieu. The guns of the left wing remained in their advantageous position on the high ground, and soon opened fire on several bodies of the enemy's cavalry which appeared on the plain in front of Frichermont.

The enemy's artillery, which sent its first volleys on our left wing (one of the first shots killing the brave Major Hegmann, in command of the 3rd Battalion Nassau), soon covered the whole of our line, but more especially directed its fire on the farmhouses of Hougoumont and La Haye Sainte.

* This paragraph furnishes the conclusive proof that the Bylandt brigade was withdrawn *before* the battle began from the ground it has been accused of abandoning in a cowardly fashion.

APPENDIX 61

One hundred and seventy thousand men with 450 guns were now engaged in a battle destined to have such an important influence on the fate of our country and also on that of France, in danger of being laid again under the iron sceptre of its impenetrable tyrant.

The attack on the left wing proved only to be an act of reconnoitring, in order to find out whether our left wing joined the Prussian troops, and whether it would be possible to turn our left flank by way of Frichermont. In the first attack the enemy made use of no other troops than those of cavalry and artillery, which were easily beaten off, after which these troops returned to regain their position in the army of the enemy. The attack on the farmhouse of La Haye Sainte, and especially that of Hougoumont, was very fierce. Every effort was made to dislodge us from these positions; Jerome Buonaparte led the attack, and with a considerable number of guns tried to make himself master of the copse at Hougoumont. Several battalions of infantry arrived to strengthen the artillery, and after much trouble they succeeded in driving our troops out of it. Our men withdrew to the farm and the garden, which the enemy now attacked with the utmost fury; General Reille, at the head of the 1st Corps d'Armée, himself led the attacks.

Buonaparte, astonished at the firm resistance of our troops, and hoping to be able to pierce our lines at some spot or other, now gave order for a general charge. Whilst the troops were being concentrated for this purpose, a heavy cannonade was directed against the whole of our line, to which our guns made a telling reply, the ground on which our artillery was placed offering greater advantages than that of the enemy. This fierce cannonading having lasted about an hour, and caused the loss of many men, at two o'clock the main body of the army began its attack. They did not bring much force to bear on our left wing, but fiercely charged the centre and the right wing, with the object of breaking through our centre. Buonaparte had chosen the First Corps, the only one which had not taken part in the previous engagements. Regiment upon regiment pressed upon La Haye Sainte; each inch of ground was defended at the cost of most precious blood. At each step dead bodies encumbered the way, but, thanks to our favourable position, the enemy was at last repulsed, in spite of the remarkable bravery displayed by him and the anxiety of his troops to succeed, which was only equalled by the cool and undaunted determination of ours to frustrate their efforts.

In the meantime three columns advanced to attack our position under command of Count d'Erlon, with the 205th Regiment at their head. The enemy crossed the ravine, where he was outside the range of our fire, and drove back the posts on our flank. Having approached us to within fifty paces, not a shot had been fired, but now the impatience of the soldiers could no longer be restrained, and they greeted the enemy with a double row of fire, who, notwithstanding, kept bravely advancing. The brigade which the enemy attacked was ranged in a double row, which prevented the free use of muskets. By cutting down a few squadrons the enemy made a gap in our ranks, through which he forced his way with his columns.

Everything which was immediately in front of him was forced to give way; but the pelotons of the wings immediately filled up the gaps, taking their places in the groups nearest to them.

The enemy had now succeeded in passing our first line, and had arrived on the plain. The second line made ready to advance against him, whilst a cavalry regiment of the English Guards came on the spot to harass him in case he was forced to retreat.

Having penetrated so far the enemy then discovered large bodies of infantry which he had not been able to see from where he was, the troops having lain flat on the ground and hidden by the hedge.

Whilst the enemy was rallying his forces in great haste the nearest troops of the second line attacked his flanks, supported in the movement by the Head of the Staff, who had been able to rally about 400 men of the troops which had been forced to retire.

They succeeded in driving the enemy back over the low-lying ground, pursuing him with the bayonet even to his own ground, he being at the same time charged by the cavalry, who made great slaughter among the French.

The Netherlands troops, carried away by their impetuosity, had gone far in advance of the English, and taken two flags from the enemy; but the flying troops of the enemy having turned their artillery upon them, all the detachments of the line returned to their old position. In this engagement the Lieutenant of the Staff (Van Haren) was killed, General Perponcher had two horses shot dead under him, and the Head of the Staff (Colonel Zuylen van Nyevelt) was wounded, and several superior officers and many non-commissioned officers and soldiers having volunteered to escort the large number of prisoners we had made, it was found necessary to reorganize the different corps on the spot, which was immediately attended to.

Whilst this happened our right wing had been attacked by the enemy in the castle of Hougoumont. He brought all his strength to bear in order to seize this important position; he even succeeded in forcing an entrance into the garden, but was immediately driven back by a regiment of English Guards. The charges made by his infantry were all unsuccessful; those of his cavalry continued on our right wing with alternate loss and advantage. Notwithstanding the enemy had been repulsed in this general attack, he continued to harass our troops on separate points, more especially at La Haye Sainte, whilst by his incessant firing many of our men were killed. It was easy for him to renew the attacks and keep up a constant firing, as he had twice as much artillery and double the men we had; it was also most important for him to secure the position before the arrival of the Prussians.

We were able to exchange messages with the latter by way of Ohain. Intelligence had been received that they were approaching, but were hampered by the bad state of the roads and detained at the defile of St. Lambert, that Prince Blucher would soon be at Jean Loo, and that General Bulow had received the order to attack the right wing of the French from the east side of that wood.

At six o'clock we heard a fierce cannonade on our left wing. General Perponcher, who till now had remained with the First Brigade in the centre of our position, thinking that his presence might be required on the left wing, went to Smohain, accompanied by the Head of the Staff.

The enemy, seeing the Prussians appear on the field, redoubled his attacks, and for a short time got possession of a few houses of Smohain and of the outhouses of the castle of Frichermont, from which he was, however, soon driven again by Major van Normann, with the 2nd Battalion Nassau; but the Prussian Tirailleurs of General Bulow, who in great numbers came from the west side of the wood lying between Jean Loo and Aywiers, mistaking the uniform of the Nassau troops for those of the French, an unfortunate incident happened. The epaulettes of the officers, the form and ornaments of the shakos, the colbacks of the Grenadiers, and the similarity of the marching and the signalling, made the Prussians believe that they were in the presence of the enemy; and they opened a heavy fire on our Tirailleurs of the left wing. As no explanation seemed possible, His Excellency the General of the Division ordered our men to retire, which they did in the best of order. A few minutes later, when matters had been explained, the men fell again into line; the company of the Grenadiers of the 3rd Battalion Nassau joined themselves to the Prussian troops, and followed their movements *en tirailleur*.

Napoleon, seeing that the troops of Bulow and probably the remainder of the Prussian army would soon envelop his right wing, had to choose between two alternatives—either to fall back or to make a desperate attack. He chose the latter. After so many failures, he had lost all hope of gaining possession of the farmhouse of Hougoumont, and as our remaining there would seriously hamper the evolutions of his cavalry, he gave orders to set fire to it, so as to force us out of it. The united efforts of several batteries were now brought to bear on this point, sending out volley after volley, with the result that the farmhouse was soon enveloped in flames. The garrison withdrew in perfect order, but unfortunately the wounded, among whom was Lieutenant Hardt, perished in the flames. Having thus gained a larger space for the operations of his left wing, he renewed the attack on the whole of the line. His artillery was moved farther forward, and made terrible havoc among our troops. Our losses became tremendous; we had no more men in reserve; every one of our soldiers was actively engaged.

The 5th Battalion National Militia had taken its place in the first line, which was advancing in the direction of the enemy, as far as the middle of the ravine, for the support of the troops which, on the left, covered the farmhouse of La Haye Sainte. The whole of the reserve artillery of the enemy had been brought together at this spot. Except for a few cavalry charges on our right wing, the enemy attacked *no other position of our line* but the centre of *our* position.

The enemy charged our troops with the greatest fury; whole battalions were cut down and immediately replaced by others. On both sides fresh regiments were being opposed to fresh regiments, which in their turn were soon so weakened that their place must be taken by others, who in their turn again must leave the place for new victims.

The smallest advantage of the ground was defended with the greatest tenacity, and the smallest obstacle, which at other times would pass unnoticed, became an object of the most serious contest, for the gaining of which the blood of conquerors and vanquished must flow in torrents.

The troops at La Haye Sainte having exhausted their ammunition, the enemy succeeded in taking possession of the farmhouse for a short time, but soon had to abandon it. On this occasion H.R.H. the Prince of Orange was wounded by a bullet at the moment when, in order to encourage his men, he rode in advance of them towards the enemy.

Towards seven o'clock in the evening, the First Brigade being exposed on the slope of the hill to the heaviest grapeshot fire, and having exhausted its cartridges, could no longer maintain itself in this position, and withdrew to the rear of the line under command of Lieutenant-Colonel de Jongh.

The corps of Prince Blucher having come to our assistance at seven o'clock, Buonaparte saw that all would be lost unless he remained master of the field. He now gave the order for a renewed attack; the pick of the French army, composed principally of Guards and commanded by the Emperor himself, led the charge; both sides fought with the utmost determination; heaps of dead bodies were lying about everywhere, but the English managed to save the position. General Bulow in the meantime having attacked the right wing of the enemy, gained considerable advantage over them, and a Division of English light cavalry and the cavalry of General Ziethen of the corps of Prince Blucher having come on the spot, our army strained every effort to gain the victory.

The cavalry of the enemy was not able to resist the charges of this fresh cavalry and was driven back. As General Bulow was already operating on the rear of the enemy's right wing, there was a moment's hesitation in the enemy's camp, of which the Duke of Wellington took advantage to order the whole line to press forward.

In a few moments the French army was completely routed; those who found no way of escape were mercilessly cut down with the sabre or bayonet; having nowhere any reserve left, the army had no point of rallying. Vehicles of all kinds encumbered the highroad, and along it, right and left, Frenchmen rushed in great confusion, pursued by the Prussians and part of our troops.

Near Genappe the enemy made a short stand; he hoped that the numerous vehicles placed at the entrance of the defile would prevent our further pursuit; his rearguard had posted a few pieces to the right and left of the road so as to cover the retreat, but our guns soon silenced them, and our infantry having made for itself a passage between the vehicles, the enemy was forced to seek safety in flight.

Some of the Tirailleurs of our troops which had been in pursuit of the enemy, finding that the English army had been relieved by the Prussians, then returned to their corps; others, exhausted by the day's work, remained at Genappe during the night, and only rejoined them on the following day.

It had now become quite dark, and the whole army lay down to rest close to the battlefield. The Division was distributed over the ground in the following way:

On the right wing the 1st Battalion Nassau, on the grounds of the farmhouse of Hougoumont; in the centre the First Brigade, against the forest of Soignes, to the left of the road to Brussels; on the left wing the Staff of the Division, with the Second Brigade on the road of Ohain to Braine l'Alleud, at the point where it is cut by the road of Ransbeck to Jean Loo. The artillery belonging to each of the wings was placed foremost, whilst four companies of the 1st Battalion Regiment No. 28 were posted in the castle of Frichermont and in the village of Smohain. The artillery belonging to the centre, for want of ammunition, had been obliged to retire, leaving a disabled gun behind for which no gun-carriage could be found; the remaining pieces had been removed to the park, with the object of replenishing the ammunition; but a false alarm and the great confusion in the rear of the army had made some of the riders lose their heads, and notwithstanding the remonstrances of their officers, they had cut the traces and joined in a general movement of retreat upon Brussels.

This had been as glorious a day for the Division as the 16th. Although it had already been two days in action, it was moved still further in the front of the first line, and it was owing to the heroism of the Netherlanders on the 16th that the corps gained the distinction of being placed, on the 18th, on the two most important points of the army, namely, in the centre and at both the extremities of the wings. During the three days the Division lost 90 officers and 2,090 men, 4 guns and 1,700 muskets; the artillery fired 1,600 shots, the infantry used 500,000 cartridges.

The losses of the entire army were, in proportion to that of the Division, but small in comparison with that of the enemy, who also lost all his baggage (comprising 300 guns), whilst as the result of the battle an army was destroyed with which the tyrant had hoped to disturb again the peace of Europe and force it to a renewed struggle against him.

June 19.—Prince Blucher having taken upon himself the pursuit of the enemy, the troops remained in camp until ten o'clock on the following morning. When they prepared for leaving, the English troops were assembled around Nivelles and the Netherlands troops on the highroad of Bois Seigneur Isac, where in the course of the day all the corps of the infantry of the Division were brought, together with two guns of the foot battery, the horse artillery having received orders not to start until the damage done to their matériel had been completely restored.

The Colonel Chief of the Staff,
(Signed) VAN ZUYLEN VAN NYEVELT.

Headquarters at St. Leu Taverney,
October 25, 1815.

GENERAL TRIP'S REPORT ON THE HEAVY CAVALRY.

Soon after the battle had commenced I was commanded by Lieutenant-General Collaert to leave my position near Mont St. Jean, and to make an advance movement. The brigade then took its stand to the right of the highroad from Mont St. Jean to Charleroi, behind some bodies of English infantry which were engaged with the enemy near that spot. Towards half-past one I received the order from Lieutenant-General Collaert to seize on every opportunity whenever there was a chance of advantageously making a charge with my brigade. After having executed a few movements which the occasion demanded, about three o'clock a superior English officer came to inform me that the enemy was preparing to march along the high-road from Charleroi, with the object of gaining Mont St. Jean. I at once placed two squadrons of the 3rd Regiment of Carabiniers in compact column on the high-road, whilst the 1st Regiment was formed in an oblique front with the intention of attacking the enemy in front and in the flank, should he succeed in approaching us. The 2nd Regiment was kept in reserve, and placed in the second line. The charge of the enemy having failed, and as I considered the presence of my brigade was no longer of use at that part, I moved further towards the right on the level of the plateau to cover the English infantry which were standing there drawn up in squares. Having remained for a few minutes in this position, I observed a body of the enemy's Cuirassiers preparing to charge the English squares. Considering this a favourable moment for an attack on the enemy's cavalry, I advanced towards them with the 1st Regiment of the Carabiniers, and drove them back into the squares of their own infantry, the enemy leaving many killed and wounded.

Whilst the 1st Regiment was rallying the enemy attempted a second charge, which was again repulsed by the 2nd and 3rd Regiments. On this occasion several French Cuirassiers fell into our hands.

After the brigade had rallied again, the men were chiefly engaged in guarding that position, or were led by me to any spot where they seemed most needed.

About half-past five I received an order from H.R.H. the Prince of Orange to take up my position behind some squares of English and Nassau troops. I remained in that position till about seven o'clock, when I was informed of the order of Lord Uxbridge, Commander-in-Chief of the Cavalry, who directed that all the cavalry should be placed on the low ground to the left of the highroad of Mont St. Jean to Nivelles, where part of the English cavalry had also been placed.

After we had taken up our position there, Lieutenant-General Collaert was wounded by the bursting of a howitzer, and gave me the command of the Netherlands cavalry, I being then the oldest Major-General, Major-General van Merlen having been mortally wounded. Here I was joined by the brigade of Major-General Ghigny, and from this time (about half-past seven) I received no further orders of any kind.

Observing the English cavalry making an advance movement, I followed the same, and during the subsequent retreat of the French army I continued to regulate my movements by those of the English cavalry.

Towards midnight I arrived with the Division at about three-quarters of an hour's distance from Genappe, and as it seemed useless to march further, the men and horses being thoroughly done up, I bivouacked there for the night.

The next day (June 19), no orders being forthcoming, I marched with the Division to Nivelles, which I reached about mid-day, and there I was informed that the Netherlands army was being concentrated at Bois Seigneur Isac, to which place I took the Division in my charge. During the morning of the 20th the 6th Regiment of Hussars, the Light Dragoons No. 5, and the mounted artillery also joined the corps.

The Major-General commanding the Brigade of Carabiniers,
(Signed)   A. D. TRIP.

GENERAL GHIGNY'S REPORT ON THE BATTLE OF MONT ST. JEAN,
JUNE 18, 1815.

At half-past eleven, when the first cannon-shots were discharged from the French line, and when the skirmishers began to make themselves heard, I gave the order at once to my brigade to 'Mount' at the spot where it was bivouacked, near the farm of Mont St. Jean, and I immediately caused it to take up a position on the right of the chaussée (Brussels to Charleroi) in the same line as a portion of the English cavalry.

About half-past two in the afternoon I perceived a retrograde movement being made by some of our troops on our left. Immediately I ordered my brigade to cross in squadrons to the left-hand side of the chaussée, whereupon I brought up the 8th Hussars to the front at a trot, followed by the 4th Light Dragoons in echelon. We caused the whole of the cavalry which was in front of us, composed of Lancers, to retire until it reached the flank of a very numerous battalion formed in square on rising ground on the further side of the ravine. Arrived at half distance from this battalion, I sounded the 'Halt.' My skirmishers were engaged with theirs, and immediately afterwards they detached a large number of sharpshooters on foot from their front, assisted by some companies which were behind them and supported by their cavalry on my left. As the enemy's fire became very vigorous, I ordered the 'Retire' by echelon. After recrossing the ravine, I took up a fresh order of battle close to the English infantry, which partly consisted of Highlanders, who were forming their line. Here the rifle and cannon fire on both sides was extremely vigorous.

General Exbricht (sic)—Lord Uxbridge—commanding in chief the English cavalry, told me twice not to quit this position under his orders, seeing that I was perfectly placed to support the infantry and artillery which were near me.

A moment later, however, I received an order to proceed with all speed on the right across the road to a point where the General-in-Chief (Wellington) ordered me to advance across the height to take up a position, where I found on my right three battalions of the English Guard in square, and on my left a regiment of Nassau infantry. A charge was at once executed against the Cuirassiers, who were repulsed.

I constantly maintained myself in this position and its proximity, manœuvring and observing the enemy's movements. My loss, as much in officers as men and horses, was during a certain time very considerable.

Towards the end of the battle I joined the Brigade of General Trip, who had assumed the chief command of our cavalry in consequence of General Collaert having been wounded. We bivouacked in front of the battle-field on the left of the Nivelles road, together with the English troops, and also with the regiment of the 5th Light Horse, which passed under my orders at this moment. On the next day we marched for the town named below.

MAJOR-GENERAL BARON GHIGNY.

ACCOUNT OF THE MOVEMENTS OF THE CAVALRY DIVISION FROM JUNE 15, 1815, TO THE MORNING OF JUNE 19 FOLLOWING.

Towards mid-day of June 15, H.R.H. the Prince of Orange commanded Major-General Van Merlen at St. Symphorien to remove his headquarters to Bray at six o'clock in the evening, after withdrawing his outposts, and to place his brigade in the following positions:

Regiment Light Dragoons, No. 5: one squadron at St. Symphorien and one at Bray.

Regiment of Hussars, No. 6: one squadron at Estienne-au-Val, one company at Maurage, one squadron at Serrone, and one company at Bray, and two pieces of mounted artillery at Maurage.

The First Brigade of Light Infantry was ordered to quit its quarters at the same hour and to bivouac behind Havre; the Brigade of Heavy Cavalry and the battery of mounted artillery were to take position behind Strepis, near L'Arbre Seul.

At five o'clock in the morning of the 16th, Lieutenant-General Baron de Collaert received an order to concentrate the Division of cavalry at Baume, to march to Arquennes, near Nivelles, and to take up his position at that place, which he did; but the brigade of General van Merlen and two pieces of mounted artillery, commanded by Captain Gey, when close to Nivelles, received an order, sent by His Royal Highness through one of his adjutants, to march to Quatre Bras, where in the afternoon of the same day he fought the enemy.

On the 17th, towards eleven o'clock in the morning, Lieutenant-General Baron de Collaert was ordered to leave his position and to retire to Mont St. Jean, viâ Nivelles, where a squadron was to be left behind to protect the removal of the baggage from that place. The Division joined at Mont St. Jean, about five o'clock in the afternoon, the brigade of General van Merlen, who had already reached that place, and bivouacked on the highroad from Nivelles and Charleroi. The squadron which had remained behind at Nivelles joined the Division in the evening.

On the 18th, a little after ten o'clock in the morning, the Division occupied the following positions in front of Mont St. Jean:

The First Brigade Light Cavalry to the right of the road to Charleroi; each regiment formed in column.

The Second Brigade Light Cavalry and the Second Brigade Heavy Cavalry arranged in the same way to the left of the road to Nivelles, the mounted artillery in the centre, placed in a line with the regiment of Carabiniers No. 3.

From the moment the battle commenced each brigade, in accordance with the order of His Royal Highness, acted on its own responsibility. I must therefore refer to the details of the several commanders, which I join herewith.

The account of Major-General Ghigny has not yet reached me, although I applied for it immediately and very urgently on October 2.

The Lieutenant-Colonel, Chief of the Staff of Cavalry,

(Signed) HOYINCK VAN PAPENDRECHT.*

A SHORT ACCOUNT OF WHAT HAPPENED DURING THE BATTLE OF JUNE 18, 1815, TO THE BATTERY OF THE MOUNTED ARTILLERY ATTACHED TO THE CAVALRY OF THE ROYAL NETHERLANDS ARMY.

After the two 6-pounder guns of the brigade of light cavalry, which was commanded by Captain Gey, had joined my battery about eleven o'clock in the morning, I received from Lieutenant-Colonel Hoyinck van Papendrecht, Chief of the General Staff of Cavalry, the order to advance with my battery, consisting of six 6-pounder guns and two 24-pounder iron howitzers, and to take up a position on the plateau of Mont St. Jean. I went thither with my battery, and took up my position to the left of the highroad of Nivelles, being supported on the right by a battery of mounted artillery, and on the left by a battery of foot artillery of the English army, which on its right joined the

* General Van Merlen having been killed, there is no report for his brigade.

APPENDIX 69

Brunswick troops. I had taken up my position opposite the farm called Hougoumont, where I at once became engaged with the enemy. From this position I continued firing until seven or eight o'clock in the evening, but owing to the loss of the greater part of the horses, which had been killed or wounded by the enemy's fire, leaving my battery almost useless, and also on account of the blowing up of three powder caissons, which had greatly diminished our ammunition, I received the order to withdraw my battery so as to allow the horses to be replaced from the reserve, to renew the harness, and then to await further orders.

Having thus removed with my battery behind the windmill of the village of Mont St. Jean, where the reserve of my battery had been left, and having replaced the teams and the destroyed ammunition as well as circumstances allowed, I was left without further orders until next day, June 19, in the morning, when I was commanded to follow with my battery the cavalry on the road to Nivelles, and further to Bois Seigneur Isac, where the entire cavalry force was united, whose movements I then followed.

The Captain commanding the Battery of Mounted Artillery attached to the Division of Cavalry.

(Signed) A. PETTER.

Sanois, October 16, 1815.

PRINCE OF ORANGE'S REPORT TO KING WILLIAM OF THE NETHERLANDS ON THE BATTLE OF WATERLOO.

Brussels, June 22, 1815.

After the battle of the 16th, of which I had the honour to give an account to Your Majesty on the 17th at two in the morning from my headquarters at Nivelles, the Duke of Wellington, in order to remain in line with the Prussian Army, made the same morning a movement, in consequence of which the army found itself at six in the evening in position on the heights in front of Waterloo, where it bivouacked. The enemy's cavalry, which followed the movements of the army, was at different times repulsed with loss by the English cavalry.

The 18th at daybreak we discovered the enemy in front of us, and at ten o'clock he commenced his dispositions for the attack. The army of Buonaparté (*sic*) was composed of First, Second, Third, Fourth, and Sixth Corps of the Imperial Guard, of almost the whole of his cavalry, and of an artillery of several hundred guns. Towards eleven o'clock the enemy unmasked a battery of a small number of pieces; under cover of this fire his Tirailleurs advanced against our right wing, and an instant later his attack was directed against a farm surrounded by a copse (*taillis*), which was situated a little in front of that wing, and to the left of the Nivelles road (that is, looking west). The enemy made, but in vain, the most furious attacks to capture this farm. At twelve the cannonade became strong, and at half-past the combat extended all along the line. The French attacked our two wings several times, but the principal object was to pierce by the right of the centre, and they employed all their means to achieve this. Columns of hostile cavalry charged us with great daring; but despite the inconceivable obstinacy with which they renewed their attacks, from half-past three till the end of the battle, they never succeeded in making our line give way. The enemy were constantly repulsed, as much by the fire of our squares as by the charges of our cavalry. It is impossible to paint for Your Majesty the fury with which they fought, especially in the six last hours. I was not happy enough to see the end of this battle, as glorious as it is important, having received half an hour before the defeat of the enemy a ball through the left shoulder, which obliged me to quit the battlefield.

It is with the liveliest satisfaction that I can inform Your Majesty that the troops of all arms fought with the greatest courage. In the cavalry charges, the brigade of the Carabiniers was particularly remarked. The Division of Lieutenant-General Chassé was only engaged late, and as I could not personally leave the centre, I had placed him for the day under the orders of Lord Hill, commanding the Second Army Corps. I have learnt that this Division also conducted itself with much valour, and that Lieutenant-General Chassé, as also his two brigadiers, perfectly performed their duty.

I have not been able up to this to inform Your Majesty in detail of the loss we have suffered, not yet having received the reports under this head. At the same time, I am obliged to state, with a profound sentiment of regret, that it is considerable. The Generals of Divisions have been charged to name to me those who were particularly distinguished, and I must in the meanwhile confine myself to naming to Your Majesty those of whose conduct I was myself a witness. These are :

Lieutenant-Generals Collaert and de Perponcher. The former is wounded.

Major-General van Merlen, a brave and experienced officer; died of his wounds on the field of battle. I seize the occasion to recommend his widow and his children to the benevolence of Your Majesty.

Major-General Trip, who was particularly distinguished as much by his intelligence as by his bravery.

Major-General Ghigny. The commanders of the three regiments of Carabiniers—viz., Lieutenant-Colonel Coenegracht—dead of his wounds—Colonel de Bruyn, and Lieutenant-Colonel Lechleitner. Lieutenant-Colonel Westenberg, commanding the 5th Battalion of Militia, who is a very good officer, and very skilfully led his battalion, which performed perfectly in the battle of the 16th, etc.

I have charged my Adjutant, Major van Hoost, to hand this report to Your Majesty, and I take the liberty of recommending him to your benevolence.

WILLIAM, PRINCE OF ORANGE.

BATTLE OF QUATRE BRAS
at 2 o'clock, p.m.

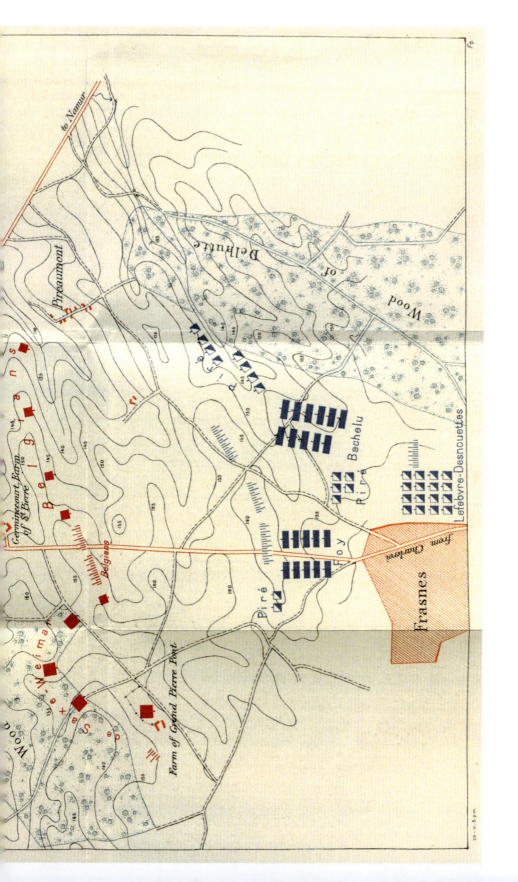

BATTLE OF QUATRE BRAS
¼ past 3 o'clock, p.m.

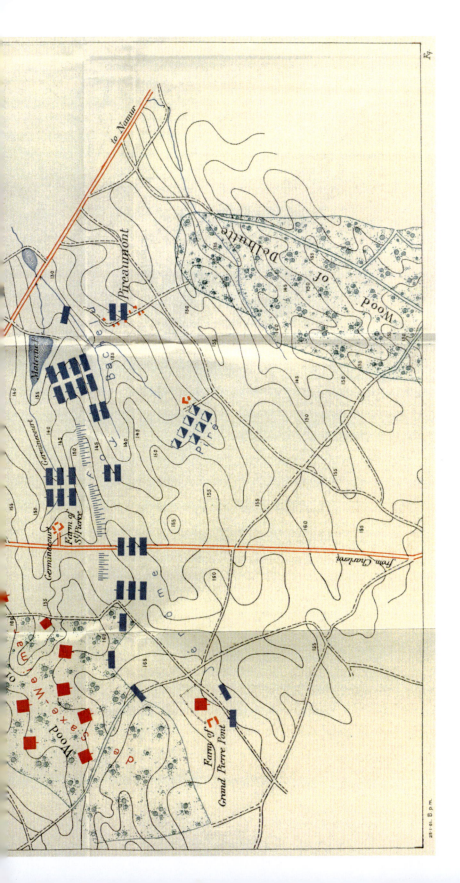

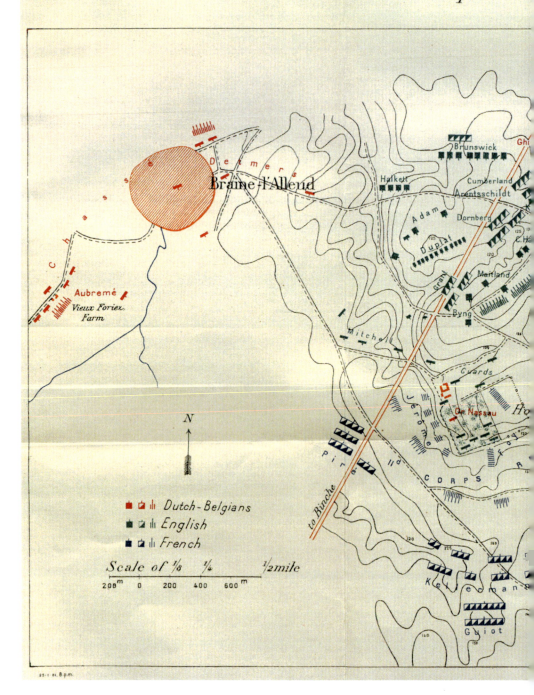

WATERLOO
clock, p.m.

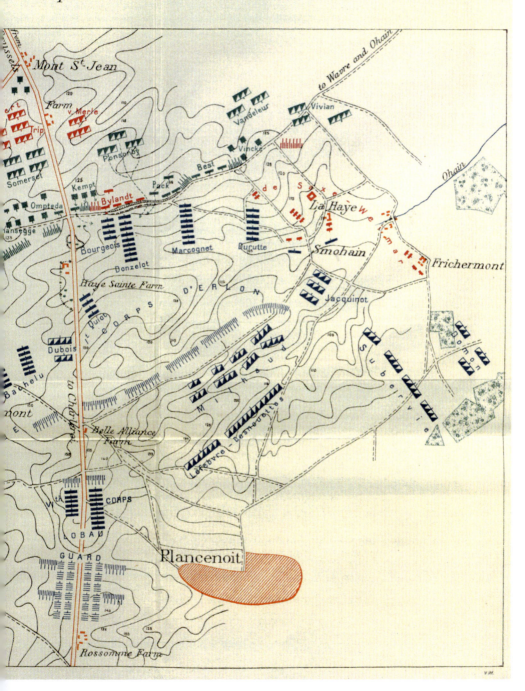

BATTLE OF WATERLOO
at 8 o'clock, p.m.

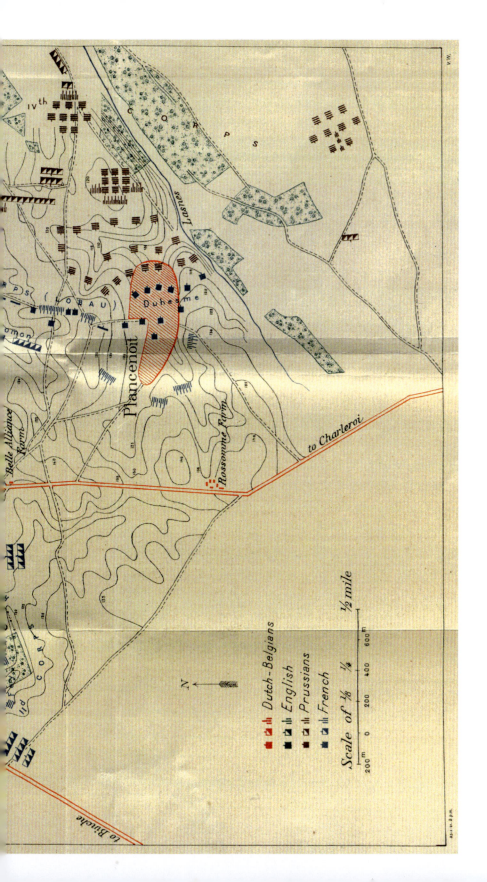